THE GREAT
RECESSION

History, Ideology, Hubris and Nemesis

THE GREAT RECESSION

History, Ideology, Hubris and Nemesis

Michael Heng Siam-Heng

East Asian Institute, National University of Singapore

World Scientific

NEW JERSEY · LONDON · SINGAPORE · BEIJING · SHANGHAI · HONG KONG · TAIPEI · CHENNAI

Published by

World Scientific Publishing Co. Pte. Ltd.

5 Toh Tuck Link, Singapore 596224

USA office: 27 Warren Street, Suite 401-402, Hackensack, NJ 07601

UK office: 57 Shelton Street, Covent Garden, London WC2H 9HE

British Library Cataloguing-in-Publication Data
A catalogue record for this book is available from the British Library.

THE GREAT RECESSION
History, Ideology, Hubris and Nemesis

ISBN-13 978-981-4313-40-7
ISBN-10 981-4313-40-8

Typeset by Stallion Press

Printed in Singapore.

In loving memory of

my eldest sister Heng Siew Cheng

and

my wife Irene Koh Siew Yin

Contents

Preface   ix

Chapter 1   Introduction   1
Chapter 2   From Berlin Wall to Wall Street   23
Chapter 3   A Tale of Two Crises   51
Chapter 4   Insights from Japan's "Lost Decade"   77
Chapter 5   Special Features of the 2008 Crisis   125
Chapter 6   Bonfire of Financial Excesses   139
Chapter 7   The Moral Economy   177
Chapter 8   A New Financial Landscape?   203
Chapter 9   Globalization and All That   225
Chapter 10   Don't Waste the Crisis   243

Index   265

Preface

The first sign of the financial crisis appeared in mid-2007. But it became a full-blown hurricane in mid-September 2008, just a few months away from the US presidential election. It happened at a time when the economy was the main concern of the American people despite its wars in Iraq and Afghanistan. The crisis has thus played an important role in swaying the undecided votes in favor of Barack Obama. Though it is still too early to sketch the profile of positive changes ahead, the world is delighted that it has a break with the Bush period. This reminds us of the Asian financial crisis that helped to bring down President Suharto of Indonesia. An ignominious downfall of the Smiling General was unthinkable before the Asian financial crisis.

Given the important role of the USA in geopolitics, the new administration of Obama brings hope to those longing for a more peaceful international order. President Obama has advocated nuclear disarmament, though it is not clear how much he can ultimately achieve on this front. The award of the Nobel Peace Prize can thus be seen as an endorsement of his efforts so far and more so as an encouragement for him and his team to press ahead.

Very few who have a deep interest in the complex and even mysterious nature of social phenomena can resist the temptation to follow closely the financial crisis and the economic recession in its wake. And to follow the events in depth while testing out formative ideas, I have decided to write this book.

I must confess that I was rather hesitant in writing the book. We are too close to the crisis to be able to pinpoint the key sub-events that contribute to it, to make sense of it and to draw its long-term implications. Some thoughtful friends have urged me to postpone the writing in order to benefit from the passage of time. The interval would provide me the historical distance needed for reflections, for speculative ideas to go through the crucible of critical examinations by evolving events. Time acts like a gravitational force attracting the weightier and more solid writings to settle down at the bottom, while letting the superficial ideas float away with the current of events. It often takes a long while before economists, sociologists, and other social scientists are able to see a deep recession in its proper perspective. Only then can they hope to separate the central issues from the side issues, and to distill lessons from them. One colleague reminded me that the economist John Galbraith published his *The Great Crash, 1929* a clean quarter century after the event. He certainly has a point. But there is the pleasure of sharing my feelings and thoughts with others, to engage the wider world in discussion and to partake of the intellectual adventure. The book you are reading is in this sense the product of an exploratory study.

Writing a book is always an instructive and humbling experience. It reminds me of how difficult it is to think clearly and logically, and even more difficult to express the thoughts coherently and succinctly in words. The writing task, though heavy, is made lighter by the continuing encouragement from my two darling daughters, Kirin and Sarina. Colleagues and friends have been very kind in supplying me with materials, ideas, and insightful comments on the various drafts. To the following colleagues and friends, I owe my deep gratitude: Abdul Rahman Embong, Charles Adams, Ishtiaq Ahmed, Chen Gang, Chen Wenbo, Chua Chieu Hiong, Sven Fischer, Hou Heng Neng, Tineke Jansen, Habibullah Khan, Kwok Chu Chin, Lam Peng Er, Lie Chen-Ie, Liem Soei Liong, Lim Mah Hui, Lim Swee Keng, Lye Liang Fook, Bhanoji Rao, Ten Chin Liew, Barnard Turner, John Wong, Yang Mu, and Yeoh Kean Ooi.

Earlier versions of Chapters 2, 4 and 5, were given respectively as talks to participants who attended my course on International Finance at Ngee Ann Polytechnic, at Singapore Institute of International Affairs and at Chinese Chamber of Commerce of Singapore. I would like to thank all the attendees.

While some of the good ideas in the book are due to input from all those I thank, I remain the one responsible for its flaws.

The East Asian Institute of National University of Singapore has provided me the environment to think and work. To EAI, my special thanks.

In bringing out this book, I am fortunate to have the cooperation of World Scientific Publishing Company. I would like to record here my appreciation for the patience and professional assistance of the editors, Ms Lim Shujuan and Ms Sandhya.

Unless otherwise stated, the dollar ($) refers to the US dollar.

Finally, could I invite you to email me your comments to help me learn from my mistakes and perhaps write another book on the topic some time in the future.

Michael HENG Siam-Heng
hsh9839@yahoo.com
31st January 2010

Chapter One

Introduction

One day of freezing cold will not produce ice one meter-thick.

— Chinese proverb

Those in key positions tend to see the world through key holes.

There is general consensus that the financial tsunami of 2008 is the worst financial crisis facing the world since the Great Depression of the 1930s. It came close to bringing down the banking system of the USA and Britain. It shook the international financial systems and subsequently pushed the world economy into a painful recession. The New York stock market plunged by 57 percent from its peak in October 2007 to its depth in March 2009. It constitutes a defining moment in the history of international financial system and economy of our life time.

Several years before the outbreak, respectable economists in the USA were warning of the danger, basing their arguments on the twin problems posed by budget deficits and trade deficits, and practices of financial excesses. Unfortunately, their warnings were ignored by the political leadership and regulatory bodies. The regulators seemed to behave like "none's so blind as those who would not see, none's so deaf as those who would not hear". Surely these authorities are staffed by some of the best and brightest. What has gone amiss? Perhaps their over-optimistic assessment of the situation was shared by the broad section of society. If so, what was the intellectual climate then?

After the crisis, key words such as dysfunctional incentive schemes, deregulation, failures of rating agencies, financial excesses, greed, easy money, and financial imbalances have appeared repeatedly in reports and analyses of the current economic crisis. These have formed the main themes of policy studies and scholarly research. All these tell a good part of the story. Some offer conceptual frameworks to tell a coherent story of the collapse.[1] Others provide detailed and juicy stories, documenting the unfolding of the key episodes of the crisis.[2] Basically, the approaches are within the framework of monetary economics or financial economics.

This book is different. It begins with the real economy. It situates the current crisis in the societal context of the last several decades and as part of social, economic, political, cultural, and intellectual changes. Financial system is part and parcel of the economic system, and financial crisis is a manifestation of the underlying problems in the economy. The crisis blew up in the backdrop of a persistent tendency toward overcapacity in the global manufacturing sector. The advanced industrial economies could have responded to it by making a quantum jump across a broad range of technologies. Instead they resorted to financial and monetary stimulations time and again. As the fundamental problem of overcapacity was not solved, each round of stimulus provided the conditions for a bubble, leading to the formation of the super-bubble, which burst in 2008. In this sense, the current recession is at its core a very serious economic crisis.

Though it is an economic crisis, we have to go beyond an economic focus to have a well-grounded understanding of it. For example, bankers, in giving free rein to their greed, have been responsible for financial excesses and reckless speculation. But greed is part of the human condition and it can only wreak havoc under certain societal conditions. This suggests that we need to look at the deregulated financial systems inspired by free market fundamentalism. The institutional setup has provided a permissive environment for financial speculation to run wild.

Declining Vitality of Advanced Industrial Economies

Many discussions of the crisis mention American trade deficits but significantly they do not use that as a point of departure to pursue the problem further. One exception is the treatment of the subject by Robert Brenner.[3] One convenient period to begin the story is the mid-1950s when Japan embarked on a state-led and export-oriented strategy to develop its economy. From mid-1950s to mid-1980s, Japan surprised the world with the most spectacular economic growth in human history. Japanese companies flooded the world market with high-quality manufactured goods. Self-confidence of the West was sapped when the German camera industry and American home appliances and machine tools industries were nearly wiped out. Until 1965 or so, these industries were thought to be without rivals.

The enormous success of the strategy was evident by the 1960s, which attracted Taiwan and South Korea to follow its footstep. Soon the two new converts were joined by other East Asian countries. The result was overcapacity in manufacturing, which led to drop in profits in advanced industrialized economies.[4] There was a brief period from 1985 to 1995 when the US manufacturing staged a revival of profitability and export growth. Besides relying on IT innovation, this revival was based on tax breaks, wage freeze, and weak dollar (as a result of the Plaza Accord in 1985). However, the revival was too short and lacked the "critical mass" to provide the dynamism and momentum for a paradigmatic transformation of the economic landscape.

The advanced industrial economies had shunned from the difficult strategy of investing in R&D in order to make a quantum jump across a *broad range* of technologies. Admittedly, there were technological breakthroughs in the case of Internet-related innovations. But these technological innovations taken together were not broad enough and they could not generate enough *new hightech* manufacturing capabilities to maintain the profit levels and provide employment of the good old days. Had they done so, they could have provided the world with more sophisticated technologies while the late comers would take over their contemporary technologies. It would have benefited the world by creating a kind of win–win international division of labor through complementary specialization of production.[5]

The failure of the advanced industrial economies to do so is an inauspicious sign of their economies and societies, in the broad sense of the term. "The basic source of today's crisis is the declining vitality of the advanced economies since 1973, and, especially, since 2000.... Most telling, the business cycle that just ended, from 2001 through 2007, was — by far — the weakest of the postwar period, and this is despite the greatest government-sponsored economic stimulus in U.S. peacetime history."[6] It is not that there were no warnings about the danger of hollowing out of manufacturing, but somehow they were ignored.[7]

As it happened, these countries resorted to easier ways out. First, their manufacturers chose to relocate their factories to East Asia, which welcomed them with tax holidays. Moreover, wages were held down by state powers, sometimes with naked police brutalities as in the case of South Korea. The manufacturing firms that remained behind deployed the time-honored method of squeezing the workers. From the mid-1970s, workers' pay increase has been lagging behind the increase in productivity.[8] In this, the business world was given a helping hand by the anti-labor policies of Prime Minister Thatcher and President Reagan. The anti-labor movement was further undergirded ideologically when the Berlin Wall collapsed in late 1989 and the subsequent ideological swing to the right.

Second, governments of the rich West maintained economic growth (and therefore capital returns) by financial and monetary expansion. For a while, traditional Keynesian measures managed to pull off the act, but over time, the approach was losing steam. To prevent the economy from sinking to a level that is politically dangerous, governments then used artificially cheap credit to boost the economy.

Third, there is a systematic move to direct resources away from the daunting project of advancing technological frontiers and building social infrastructure to the finance, insurance, and real estate (FIRE) sectors where quick money can be made. In America, the financial sector's share of total corporate profits climbed from 10 percent in the early 1980s to an incredible 41 percent at its peak in 2007; the profits in the past decades are in the order of trillions.[9] Its share of the stock market's value grew from 6 percent to 23 percent. Such figures prompt even the pro-free market *The Economist* to comment: "It is hard to believe that financial services create enough value to command such pre-eminence in the economy. At the peak, the industry accounted for only 14% of America's GDP and a mere 5% of private-sector jobs."[10]

Financial speculation has also become part of the toolkits of industrial and commercial companies, whose senior executives are increasingly obsessed with deal-making. Their constant concern is merging and de-merging, buying and selling bits of their corporate portfolios.[11] The treasury department of some companies has even been actively involved in writing derivatives or in currency trading as a way to earn the extra dollar. "For a long time now a number of companies have seen their treasury areas as profit centres."[12] There are several giant companies that disappeared from the corporate world because of this. Unless the very top of the companies are snoozing most of the time, it is hard to believe that financial transactions of such nature are conducted without their knowledge.

Along the way, the day of reckoning was postponed. It is like doing patch work to cover up cracks in the structure of a bridge that needs a major repair. While the bridge looks good after each patch work, the degeneration of the structure continues unabated. The apparent success of each patch work actually increases the cost of the major repair, until of course on one fine day the bridge simply gives way. The analogy is not to dismiss the merits of patch work. But by its very nature, patch work is a temporary measure to cope with an urgent task, to win time to do the more fundamental renovation. Every good engineer knows this point.

To Wall Street's great delight, ingredients needed for the patch work — cheap money for the FIRE sector and fiscal deficits — are available. One source is from the foreign reserves of oil-exporting countries. Another is from Asian countries, which have built up massive foreign reserves as a defensive measure after the Asian financial crisis.

From Washington's perspective, it is fine that Asian countries are keeping their surpluses in US dollar and therefore in the US banking system. It allows America to afford cheap credit that delivers two advantages. Cheap credit is translated into asset booms, creating enormous profits for asset owners. Businesses can use their inflated assets to borrow more money to expand or to raise more capital by selling stocks at good prices. Assets-owning households experience the "wealth effect" and they can afford a spending binge. We have thus a period of consumption-driven growth buttressed by constant supply of cheap money. "One has therefore witnessed for the last dozen years or so the extraordinary spectacle of a world economy in which the continuation of capital accumulation has come *literally* to depend upon historic waves of speculation, carefully nurtured and publicly rationalized by state policy makers and regulators — first in equities between 1995 and 2000, then in housing and leveraged lending between 2000 and 2007. What is good for Goldman Sachs — no longer GM — is what is good for America."[13] Brenner calls this "stock market Keynesianism".

The world was given a classic example of stock market Keynesianism in the form of Japan's response to its economic difficulties in the mid-1980s. Its results are well documented — in the form of a long recession in Japan, widely known as the "lost decade". What the West had suffered at the hands of Japan was experienced by Japan then. By mid-1980s, South Korea, Taiwan, and other East Asian countries had become Japan's star pupils, if not clones. And like the West, Japan failed to make breakthroughs across a range of technologies so that it could create new industries. For sure, there were numerous incremental improvements of existing technologies, resulting in better qualities of existing products. But such ripple-like innovations are quickly copied by the newly industrialized countries that have the advantage of lower costs of production. Though exporting manufacturers of Japan were still making profits, they were facing stiff competition from the newcomers. The problem of Japan took a turn for the worse when in 1985–1986 an appreciating yen reduced its exports, put pressure on prices and profits. To ward off the downturn, the Bank of Japan slashed interest rates and orchestrated banks and brokerages firms to direct the easy money to stock and housing markets. The downturn was bought off at the price of a super-size bubble that burst in 1990. The damage to the economy and society still lingers on today, prompting some to remark that it is not one but two decades lost.

Hubris

To have a more detailed look at how the recent crisis actually unfolded in the US, it is relevant to look at deregulation and its background. Deregulation of financial markets began in the 1950s, but until the 1970s, there was not much change. Deregulation in Europe and the OECD member countries in the 1970s and 1980s was followed by financial innovation, consolidation at home, forays abroad, and some change in standards.[14] By the early 1990s, the regulatory system has largely disappeared. It is either abandoned through the formal repeal of laws or through getting around it by means of clever innovations. Financial crisis becomes a regular feature in economic life.[15] There is the credit crunch of 1966, Wall Street crash of 1987, and the collapse of the Savings and Loan in 1990. The crises from Mexico (1994) to East Asia (1997), Russia (1998), and Brazil (1999) are shocking in their frequency, virulence, contagion, and scale. The crises highlight how interconnected and vulnerable the world's financial systems have become.[16]

These crises have not really shaken the rich Western countries to serious rethinking. In the US, past recoveries from financial meltdowns gave policy makers the confidence that the Fed was very much in control.[17] Though some lessons were learned, the crises have not been used as opportunities to draw deeper lessons and to build more robust and resilient financial systems. Neither did they look at the root of the problems in the real economy. Serious structural problems in the economy were left to fester. Hubris grows. Financial excesses get worse. "The current crisis originated in the subprime mortgage market. The bursting of the US housing bubble acted as a detonator that exploded a much larger super-bubble that started developing in the 1980s when market fundamentalism became the dominant creed. That creed led to deregulation, globalization, and financial innovations based on the false assumption that markets tend toward equilibrium."[18]

Belief in near-perfect operations of the market is one of the schools of thought in market economy. Markets are known to have failed time and again. But somehow the intellectual climate developed in such a way as to favor market fundamentalism. Do democracies not allow free contest of ideas and ideologies? This leads to the question: how does this come about? The study brings into the picture the fall of the Berlin Wall, the bursting of the Japanese bubble, the dot-com boom, and the 1997 Asian financial crisis. These important events conspire to boost the standing of the Anglo-American variant of free market economy. Free market triumphalism emerged to dominate the scene, most profoundly in the world of finance.

Market Society

The term "financial excesses" has appeared repeatedly in the voluminous writings on the Wall Street collapse. Looking back, it is easy to assess the roles of Chuck

Prince of Citigroup, Sir Fred Goodwin of Royal Bank of Scotland, Richard Fuld of Lehman Brothers, and Stan O'Neal of Merrill Lynch. But before the bubble burst, they were seen as heroes, as masters of the universe. They were cheer leaders who nudged their teams to charge on and make the best of the moment. Alan Greenspan was the great high priest in the temple of neoliberalism and was an idol worshiped by the financial world. It is not wrong to see them in bad light now, given what they have done. But a more fruitful approach is to see them as products of the environment. Without the institutional setup and social attitudes, they, or at least not so many of them, would not have been able to operate on the scale they did. Seen in this light, the current financial crisis is not simply a case of villains such as Madoff and Stanford. It is not simply a case of lack of integrity of bankers either. It is not just a case of lack of oversight or an inadequacy in the design of financial systems. It is all these combined and more, including the wide acceptance of putting profits before everything else.[19] It reflects a sea change in social values, norms, culture, economic behavior, and social life. In the midst of the change, market economic fetishism spreads and has come to dominate the running of non-business organizations. In the words of Professor Michael Sandel, we have a market society.[20]

As in the past and certainly more so this time, the crisis has produced calls to reform the financial system. So far, the signs are not encouraging. There is no attempt to reduce the size of the financial sector and no attempt to break up banks that are "too big to fail". Proposals to regulate derivatives appear half-hearted, as evidenced by not banning naked credit default swaps. We can therefore understand why pessimists are predicting that we should expect another crisis in the near future.

Accountability is an important concept in social life, and certainly so in the business world. What transpired in the banking sector can hardly be used to inspire confidence in the accountability of American business system. It is surprising that in spite of the size of the crisis and the damage inflicted to the economy and society, there is hardly any move to attribute the blame and punish those responsible. "What has happened to accountability?" even teenage children are asking. One colleague remarks, "Given the scale of the crisis, it is a rather blameless crisis. It is truly amazing!" Except for the special case of Madoff, top bankers are allowed to keep their fabulous pay and bonuses even though they are mainly responsible for having driven their banks over the cliff.

The crisis has also provided a forum to argue for bringing back the moral elements in economic life. The call harks back to Plato and Aristotle who maintain that economy is part of society and economic development must serve social development. Contrary to the view advanced by neoliberalism, market economy has a lot to do with social welfare of the people, moral fabrics of society, and the social institutions based on them. It is thus instructive to study carefully the works of theory builders of market economy such as Adam Smith, Arthur Pigou, John Stuart Mill, and Alfred Marshall.

Nemesis and a Good Crisis

At the World Economic Forum in Davos early 2009, there was talk of not wasting this good crisis. It may sound bizarre to perceive the deep and painful economic crisis as a good crisis. Well, in a way it is. The crisis is a good thing at least in the sense that it is a sharp and loud wakeup call, that it provides an occasion for us to reflect hard on the underlying causes so that we are wiser for the experience. If we are not to waste this crisis, then we should look at it as the eruption of a serious disease in the body of economy and society. If the crisis marks the turn on a better path to the future, then future historians will be able to tell a story with a happy ending. Below are some points to be put on the agenda.

A good starting point to see the global economic crisis is to take a step back and take stock of the features of the new economic and social landscape. The economic world has been radically transformed since the end of World War II. Yet, we are still depending on the key institutions crafted more than 60 years ago. These institutions continue, albeit in modified forms, to carry out governance duties of global finance. Since the breakup of Bretton Woods in 1973, financial crises tend to increase in numbers and severity. It suggests that reform is sorely needed.

To start at the basics, we must be realistic in expecting the level of profits that can be generated by the corporate world. Pressure and tricks can yield exceptional profits in the short run while they create long-term problems. The foundation of economic well-being lies in adding values and increasing productivity.

The Anglo-American version of market economy has left behind some very disturbing social problems. This is most evident in drug abuse, high crime rate, and prison population in the US.[21] They are the social counterpart of ecological degradation. Between them, these problems are a kind of "societal deficits". Something very similar to nation-building must be done for societies. Just as much as we must take care of our natural resources, we must take care of our societal resources — in the form of values, human resources, and social institutions. Besides pumping money to build physical infrastructure and to clean up the environment in an effort to revive the economy, resources must also be channeled to society-building. If the crisis can lead to an effective action for society-building, then it is indeed a blessing in disguise. We can proudly record in our history book that we have not wasted the good crisis.

How do we resolve the economic problems of advanced industrial countries when their manufacturing industries are moving to low-cost late comers? For some time, the solution appeared to reside in the service sector, for example banking and financial sectors. The financial sector appears to be the information economy par excellence. It employs many people; it uses IT as the work-horse to process data and it spurs economic growth. The crisis has shown that much of it is hot air. We have to rethink what exactly information economy is and how to harness technologies for economically productive and socially useful purposes.

Major financial crisis tends to stimulate technical changes and technological innovations. If there is a quantum jump across a range of technologies, it leads to new industries, greater productivity, new products, services, organizational forms, industries, and social organizations. If that happens, a crisis can be the prelude to a long-term growth. But this cannot be assumed. Using history as guide, we need technological change, financial stability, and social progress as conditions for it. Governments can play a positive role in the process.

There is another very fundamental social trend that argues for an enhanced role for the state. It is the trend of demography. Though Japan may represent an extreme case, it does indicate what is in store for many countries in the future. Assuming that the economic wealth produced by each working person remains the same, a smaller working population will mean a smaller GDP, as the population ages and the birth rate falls below replacement rate. Left alone to the market forces, the trend of falling birth rate will continue. Similarly, market forces make it difficult for senior citizens to be employed. Healthcare for all the citizens is another issue that demands State attention. At the level of practical politics, the argument of "small state, big market" goes against social trends. It is disastrous and pure folly to pursue a policy that goes against a social trend as powerful as demographic change.

Other Questions

1. The manufacturing capacity of China, together with those existing currently elsewhere, is more than enough to meet the global demand for manufactured goods. Even before the crisis, it would imply that China might be the last country to rely on export of manufactured goods to drive its economic development. This point is now brought forward by the pressing needs of the USA to reduce its trade deficits. The question for India, Brazil, and Indonesia is: what kind of strategy can they

follow to promote economic growth and industrialization? This is an exciting time for creative thinkers among developmental economists.

2. Globalization assumes treating the whole world as one entity, especially in economic activities. This historical trend has been gathering speed since the early 1990s. There have been less restricted movements of people and trade, but the freest of all is the flow of capital. In this sense, the financial sector is the most advanced form of globalization. The catastrophic mess created by financial speculation has raised questions about globalization — its benefits as well as its nature and future. Some opine that globalization will beat a retreat.[22] This is unlikely. It will continue to roll on, but its forms and substance are likely to change. What are the new forms and content of globalization in the coming years?

3. The recession means also a shift of global balance of power. It is a shift away from a world where the US calls the shots to a more multi-polar world with the US still being the most powerful player. Change is the permanent feature of all kinds of systems. It offers the opportunity for fresh ideas. One of these is to argue for a new world order built on friendly competition and productive collaboration. Viewed in this light, the dichotomy of "the Asian century" and "the American century" is false, and has the potential for making trouble rather than doing good. But would world leaders have the wisdom and leadership to craft a new and better world order?

4. In the 1990s when China, India, and the ex-Soviet bloc joined the capitalist world, the global labor pool

grew from 1.5 billion to 3 billion.[23] The labor force in the rich world would have to learn fast to live in a new world with fierce competition. At the same time, it means the appearance of growing markets for all kinds of goods and services. From system viewpoint, their entry into the global capitalist economy represents a dramatic "shock" to the system. It is bound to cause strains and to have profound repercussions in various components of the system. However, it also means the possibility of more resources and capabilities to cope with problems of a global nature. Given the magnitude of this "shock", it is reasonable to expect more challenges ahead. For scholars of world system, the financial crisis may be seen as an important episode in the evolution of a potentially new system.

Structure of the Book

The rest of the book is organized as follows. Chapter 2 provides the background of the shift of ideological fashion after the fall of the Berlin Wall and how this has affected the financial sector. Seen in this light, it is part of the broader societal change where the reckless bankers are actors.

The collapse of the Berlin Wall at the end of 1989 represents a new milestone in the history of finance. Neoliberalism began to exert increasing influence. Chapter 3 dwells on the 1994 Mexican peso crisis and the 1997 Asian financial crisis. The two crises displayed some distinct features that are relevant for us to understand the 2008 crisis. The Mexican crisis was described by the then head of the IMF Michel Camdessus as the first financial crisis of the 21st century.

Chapter 4 looks at the Japanese bubble that burst in 1990 and its effects are still felt today. There are a few good reasons to study Japan's crisis in detail because it bears some deep similarities with America's and UK's trouble before the 2008 crisis. Japan's "lost decade" as a result of its bubble has been often invoked as a metaphor in the debates on the current recession.

Chapter 5 lists out some salient features that make the 2008 crisis so different from the others we have experienced in our lifetime.

Financial crises are generally preceded by financial excesses. Chapter 6 looks at some attributes of the financial excesses during the good times before the subprime bubble burst.

Chapter 7 argues that the global financial system is grossly unfair. As recognized by some bankers, the system fails to protect millions of innocent people who play no part in causing the crisis. In the best of ancient Greek tradition, economic development should be seen as part of social development. Finance is here to serve economy and not the other way round.

Chapter 8 gives several important ideas on how finance must be reformed to serve economy — to return to its proper role in allocating financial resources to promote socially useful and economically productive consumption and investment.

Chapter 9 discusses the recession in the context of current global situation: nature of Keynesian stimuli, geopolitical impact of the crisis, reduced intellectual influence of Uncle Sam, and in spite of talks to the contrary, American economy is still strong.

Chapter 10 lists the important reasons why the recovery is likely to be weak and slow. However, the crisis can serve as a wake-up call for the advanced economies to go back to the basics, to revamp and reform their economies to lay solid foundations for sustained economic development.

Endnotes

1. See for example, Michael Lim Mah Hui and Lim Chin (2010). *Nowhere to Hide: The Great Financial Crisis and Challenges for Asia.* Singapore: ISEAS.

2. See for example, Andrew R Sorkin (2009). *Too Big to Fail: The Inside Story of How Wall Street and Washington Fought to Save the Financial System — and Themselves,* London: Allen Lane.

3. Robert Brenner (2003). *The Boom and the Bubble: The US in the World Economy,* London: Verso.

   Robert Brenner (2006). *The Economics of Global Turbulence,* London: Verso.

   Murphy R Taggart (2009). In the Eye of the Storm: Updating the Economics of Global Turbulence, An Introduction, *The Asia-Pacific Journal, 49-1-09.*

   Brenner Robert P and Jeong Seong-jin (2009). Overproduction not Financial Collapse Is the Heart of the Crisis: The US, East Asia, and the World, *The Asia-Pacific Journal,* 7 February.

4. According to efficient market theory, overcapacity cannot occur because markets will regulate themselves. A business

facing declining profits will either disappear or switch to other business. Reality gives us ample examples of overcapacity in the form of low occupancy rates in hotels and manufacturers operating on profit margin so low that they are on the brink of bankruptcy. Indicators of overcapacity are well known to business people — depressed profits, factories working below full capacities, distributors demanding hefty discounts, and so on.

See the following references for some ideas on overcapacity. More articles on the subject can be found by using Google.

James Crotty (2002). Why There is Chronic Excess Capacity — The Market Failures Issue, *Challenge*, November–December [accessed on 20 January 2010]. Available at http://findarticles.com/p/articles/mi_m1093/is_6_45/ai_95629325/.

Wikipedia (2010). Capacity Utilization [accessed on 20 January 2010]. Available at http://en.wikipedia.org/wiki/Capacity_utilization.

Mark DeWeaver (2009). China's Excess-Capacity Nightmare, [accessed on 22 January 2010]. Available at http://www.project-syndicate.org/commentary/deweaver2/English.

5. Robert Brenner (2003).
6. Brenner, Jeong (2009).
7. One book that argues strongly for the case of reviving manufacturing is: Stephen S Cohen and John Zysman (1988). *Manufacturing Matters: The Myth of the Post-Industrial Economy*, New York: Basic Books.
8. Paul Krugman (2007). Who Was Milton Friedman? *The New York Review of Books*, 54(2), 15 February.

9. What Next? *The Economist*, 20 September 2008.

    Robert Guest (2009). The Coming Recovery, *The Economist*, 30 May 2009.

10. Edward Carr (2009). Fixing Finance, *The Economist*, 24 January 2009.

11. John Kay (1996). *The Business of Economics*, Oxford: Oxford University Press, p. 147.

12. PJ Rutterman (1995). Financial Fragility and Supervision: A Discussion. In *Coping with Financial Fragility and Systemic Risk*, HA Benink (ed.), Boston: Kluwer Academic Publishers, p. 293.

13 Brenner and Jeong (2009).

14. Charles Kindleberger (1993). *A Financial History of Western Europe*, 2nd Edition, Oxford: Oxford University Press, p. 447.

15. Gary Dymski and Robert Pollin (1994). *New Perspectives in Monetary Macroeconomics: Explorations in the Tradition of Hyman P. Minsky*, Ann Arbor: University of Michigan Press.

16. Paul Blustein (2001). *Chastening: Inside the Crisis that Rocked the Global Financial System and Humbled the IMF*, New York: Public Affairs.

17. Every time America recovers from a financial crisis, the event provides evidence both for the threat of financial crisis and for its ability to cope with it. People such as Alan Greenspan will emphasize the point that the danger is avoided, thus the reality of safety in the guise of danger. People such as George Soros will emphasize how close the economy is near the cliff of disaster, thus the reality of danger in the guise of safety.

    The paragraph is a liberal paraphrase of James March *et al.* in their discussion of plane collision in the context of organizational learning. "...every time a pilot avoids a collision, the event provides evidence both for the threat and for its irrelevance. It is not clear whether the learning should emphasize how close the organization came to a disaster, thus the reality of danger in the guise of safety, or the fact that disaster was avoided, thus the reality of safety in the guise of danger." pp. 13–14.

James G March, LS Sproull and Michal Tamuz (1996). Learning from Samples of One or Fewer, In *Organizational Learning*, Michael D Cohen and Lee S Sproull (eds.), London: Sage.

18. George Soros (2008). Regulation Revisited, 1 December [accessed on 15 January 2009]. Available at http://www. project-syndicate.org/commentary/soros39.

19. Michael Lim Mah Hui and Lim Chin (2010).

20. Michael J Sandel (2009). 2009 BBC Reith Lectures — A New Citizenship. Available at http://www.bbc.co.uk/ programmes/b00729d9.

21. Far Too Many Americans Are Behind Bars, 4 April 2009, The Economist.

22. Roger C Altman (2009). Globalization in Retreat. *Foreign Affairs*, 88(4), 2–7.

23. The Left's Resignation Note, The *Economist*, 13 December 2008.

Chapter Two

From Berlin Wall to Wall Street[a]

As a result of the experiences gained in the Great Depression, and the need to reorganize the economy to meet the new challenges arising from World War II, the USA and other western economies introduced many regulations. They were useful then. But over time a number of them proved to be a burden. In the 1970s, there was a chorus of demands from the business world to roll back the regulation and to swing back to laissez faire policies. A tireless and brilliantly effective voice was Nobel laureate of economics Milton Friedman who contributed an intellectual dimension to the campaign.[1]

Since 1976, in the background of manufacturing overcapacity and declining profits, such neoliberal ideas of economics were gaining wider acceptance.[2] An important political milestone was reached when Mrs. Margaret Thatcher came to power in 1979. She worked tirelessly to clip the wings of the British trade unions, to privatize key industries under state control, and to introduce a series of pro-business policies. In the USA, she had her counterpart and admirer in the person of Mr. Roland Reagan,

---

[a]A shorter version of the first part of this chapter appeared under the same title in *The Straits Times*, Singapore, on 26 June 2009.

who entered the White House in 1980. Both of them fervently believed in "small government, big market," and used the power of office to realize their ideals. Though Reagan was known as the champion of deregulation in the USA, in reality the deregulation movement began with the administration of his predecessors. President Gerald Ford and President Jimmy Carter both introduced deregulations in transport, communications, pipelines, savings banks and utilities. Deregulation of the financial market began even earlier in the 1960s and was continued by them.[3] As doing away with rigid regulations resulted in better economic performance, policy makers believed that the less regulations, the better. Eventually, they started to believe that self-regulation by the financial system was best; but that means no regulation for a substantial part of the financial sector.[4]

To Thatcher and Reagan, governments and the public sectors were the problem; market and business were the solution. By emancipating business from troublesome shackles of rigid regulations, both of them gained much popularity as a result of their success in promoting economic growth. The reform had its social costs in the form of job losses, and they had to deal with opposition from trade unions and the left. At the same time, they encountered strong resistance in rolling back the state. They had to contend with the reality of well-run and prosperous social democratic countries in Western Europe, the success story of Japan, and the rapidly growing economies of the Little Dragons and Tigers of East Asia. In these countries, the states played a big role.[5] More importantly, there was the Soviet Union with its allies. For nearly a century, the Soviet Union provided an alternative model.

Its emergence from a serf economy into an industrial powerhouse within a few short decades fascinated many. No one with a good sense and knowledge of history, including staunch anti-communists, can deny the crucial role of the Soviet Union in defeating Nazism in Europe. Its achievements served as a powerful source of inspiration for the newly independent countries like India.[6] Until the end of the Cold War, the Soviet Union was not seen to be far inferior to the USA. In fact, it was the only challenger to America for global hegemony. "There was a general belief that even though the Soviet Union and its allies were laggards economically, they were catching up to the wasteful market economies of the West."[7]

From the viewpoint of contest of ideas, this tug-of-war was a healthy state of affairs. However, the balance was tilted in favor of the USA with the fall of the Berlin Wall in November 1989.

The Collapse of the Berlin Wall

There are so few moments in contemporary politics that are so unhappily soaked in history and symbols as the Berlin Wall.[8] The building of the Wall was an important episode in the Cold War. It was a primary expression of the *de facto* division of the European continent between the two superpowers. To the Germans, it symbolized the division of their beloved country.

Given its background, it comes as no surprise that the spontaneous breaching of the Berlin Wall on 9 November 1989 carries so much meaning with it. The demolition of the Wall represents a potent symbol of the demise of the Soviet Union and its allies. It symbolizes that the defeat of what they embodied in terms of ideology, institutions and practices. The demise of the Berlin Wall marked the end of the Cold War and the beginning of a period of geopolitical optimism. The Soviet empire disintegrated, Germany was unified, and Europe began its movement towards a common currency.[9]

It has also tilted the economic and ideological debate between free market economy and centrally planned economy in favor of the former. In such an intellectual climate, the Anglo-American variant of free market capitalism came to gradually dominate the modus operandi of western financial markets, banks and financial firms.

Alan Greenspan observes, "The defining moment for the world's economies was the fall of the Berlin Wall in 1989, revealing a state of economic ruin behind the iron curtain far beyond the expectations of the most knowledgeable Western economists. Central planning was exposed as an unredeemable failure; coupled with and supported by the growing disillusionment over the interventionist economic policies of the Western democracies, market capitalism began quietly to displace those policies in much of the world. Central planning was no longer a subject for debate."[10]

That is fine and good. But it has gone too far to pave the way for the unchallenged march of the Anglo-American brand of free market economy. It marks the beginning of unreflective triumph of market fundamentalism, the demoralization of social democracy, the retreat of the state and the dominance of the Washington Consensus. To quote the words of George Soros: "But just because something is imperfect, the opposite is not perfect. So because of the failures of socialism, communism, we have come to believe in market fundamentalism, that markets are perfect; everything will be taken care of by markets."[11]

The results are mixed, and the world is now experiencing some of the worst consequences. In the midst of numerous newspaper reports and commentaries on the financial crisis, one article with the title *Anglo-American Capitalism on Trial* in *The New York Times* stands out. It informs us that among some of those who worked through the boom years in the City of London, the moment when matters began to get out of hand can be dated to the collapse of the Soviet Union. "One result, these people now say, was an American triumphalism that translated, in the financial world, to the kind of free-for-all."[12]

Perhaps, we can paraphrase the prescient words of the Duke of Wellington (1769–1852) after his defeat of Napoleon in the Battle of Waterloo: Next to a battle lost, the greatest danger is a battle gained.[13]

For most people, this is after-the-fact type of wisdom. Those people who were in possession of such insight two decades ago were in the minority. The neoliberal or laissez faire ideology was gradually taking deep roots in the corridors of power in various corners of the world.

Japan's Bubble, Internet Boom and Asian Crisis

To have a more complete story of the ascent of the neoliberal thinking, we have the additional stories of the Japanese bubble, the Asian financial crisis and the dot-com boom. These happened soon after the collapse of the

Berlin Wall. Between them, they enhance the American version of free market economic model.

First is the collapse of the Japanese stock and property market in 1990. From the end of the Second World War until 1990, Japan's economy was growing at a rapid rate. Given its size and growth rate, Japan was *the rising star* in the global economic scene and there was talk of Japan becoming number one, and poised to overtake America. When this would happen was only a matter of time. However, the long recession that followed the collapse of the bubble changed the whole picture drastically. It exposed grave macroeconomic blunders and structural problems. There was no more mention of the Japanese challenge. Following the Soviet Union, another contender to American dominance disappeared from the world stage.

Second is the Asian financial crisis which broke out in 1997. Before the crisis, the ASEAN group of countries was enjoying economic boom; their macroeconomic record was way above the rest of the world. In fact, their performance was the basis for the World Bank to publish the volume *The East Asian Miracle: Economic Growth and Public Policy* in 1993. Like Japan, the ASEAN countries followed a state-led model of economic development. Though it is not a Soviet style model of central planning, it is not the Anglo-American model of laissez faire economy either. To explain the role of the State in economic life and the nature of their political systems, some ASEAN countries advanced the idea of Asian Values. The idea emerged as a plausible alternative to market fundamentalism in the post Cold War period. But the Asian financial crisis put an end to the Asian Values thesis and the US variant of capitalism emerged triumphant. For the

Third World countries, the economic performance of the ASEAN countries would offer an attractive alternative to the American model. This model received a bitter beating as a result of the crisis.

Third, at the time when Japan was mired in its "lost decade," America was enjoying a decade-long economic boom led by information technology innovations. Microsoft and Intel became giant concerns. New corporate players like Yahoo!, eBay, Amazon, Cisco, Dell and Red Hat appeared. They deployed the Internet and the web technology to create new business models. A McKinsey study found that three sectors that contributed most to American productivity growth between 2000 and 2003 were retailing, wholesaling and administrative and support services.[14] These are sectors where IT had been deployed for decades, therefore accumulating much valuable experience. Wal-Mart is a well-known example in the retail sector. They possessed some key features of Schumpeterian creative destruction. Together, they remade the economic landscape. They demonstrated the vigor and vitality of American business culture and entrepreneurial spirit.

What was interesting was that the boom occurred without the expected inflationary pressure. Cheap imports, workers' hesitation to demand higher wages, and use of IT to increase productivity are often cited to explain the phenomenon. A new term was coined — borrowed from the fairy tale — the Goldilocks economy; it is not cold and not hot, just right. Another new term is "The Great Moderation."

Another contributing factor to the prosperity comes from the peace dividends. The end of the Cold War contributed to the prosperity in the 1990s in a fundamental and structural way — in the form of peace dividend. Defense spending as a share of the nation's GDP dropped by 2.6 percent. This bonanza allowed private consumption to grow rapidly and helped the Clinton administration to balance the nation's books.[15]

This series of events were perceived as manifestations of the political and economic superiority of free market ideology. Either out of cynical self interests or missionary zeal reminiscent of Kipling's "the white man's burden," the USA made use of every opportunity to spread the gospel of Washington Consensus.

By the turn of the century, a large number of influential people have been converted to the neoliberal economic thinking. "It is a change in the intellectual climate that this happened — a remarkable transformation of the conventional wisdom."[16] By any measure — protectionism versus free trade; regulation versus deregulation; wages set by collective bargaining and government minimum wages versus wages set by the market — the world has moved a long way in the direction advocated by neoliberal economists like Milton Friedman.[17]

Inroads Made by Neoliberal Thinking in Russia and China

After the fall of the Berlin Wall, Wall Street began to connect with Soviet reform circles. Russian president Boris Yeltsin was welcomed to New York and was invited by New York Fed to speak at a dinner of some 50 bankers, financiers, and corporate chiefs.[18]

The subsequent reform instituted by Moscow was very much in line with the recommendations originating from the USA and the whole world can testify to how disastrous the results are.

Luckily, China was more cautious and it declined to take the route chosen by the Russian leadership. Though China obviously made its own choice, it too drew ideological inspiration from neoliberal thinking which climbed to commanding heights after November 1989. Anglo-Saxon neoliberal thinking came into vogue in China's academia in 1992.[19] This was in the aftermath of the famous inspection tour by China's de facto leader Deng Xiaoping in the coastal free trade zones in the south. Impressed by what he saw, he urged the Chinese people to follow the example of the free trade zones, to embrace market economy and to get rich. The call is a well considered response to the problems facing the leadership after the Tiananmen Square protests in June 1989. China must speed up the economic reform in order to enlarge the economic cake and to provide employment to preempt future social unrest. "The central task is to develop the economy and the rest will take care itself." This creed is very much in line with neoliberal thinking. Chinese neoliberal scholars and policymakers are on the same wavelength with their peers in the Western world, especially the United States. They stress the economic benefits of unfettered markets, privatization of state enterprises, and a minimalist state role. Neoliberals have enthusiastically embraced China's integration with the world economy, especially after its accession to the World Trade Organization in

2001. Keith Joseph and Enoch Powell and liberal economists such as Friedrich Hayek and Milton Friedman have a large following among Chinese intellectuals and policy makers.

Retreat of the States and Ageing Population

What Mr Reagan and Mrs Thatcher failed to do in rolling back the states was accomplished for them by the Berlin Wall collapse. From that fateful day on 9 November 1989, pressure was building up for governments in many parts of the world to embark on tax reduction, deregulation, privatization and cutting back of traditional roles of governments. Private firms are allowed to operate healthcare services like hospitals, to set up schools and universities, and to run prisons.

All these were taking place in the midst of demographic change. With an ageing population, the demand for pension funds to provide for the old people grew. With retreat of the state, governments have fewer roles to play and they cut back taxes. With less sources of government revenue, governments slashed public borrowings, greatly reducing the amount of government bonds. Pension funds were either handled over to independent agencies or privatized. Other investment funds stepped in to offer pension fund services. As the quantity of government bonds shrunk, pension funds and other investment funds began to increase their portfolio in other forms of securities. They dabbled first in corporate stocks and bonds, and gradually moved into more risky investment categories like hedge funds and derivatives.

There is an increasing domination of economic life by professional fund managers whose sole purpose is to maximize profits over a short period, thus encouraging herd behavior, as pointed out by George Soros.[20] This trend represents a new source of instability in the explosive growth, especially in the United States, of share ownership through mutual funds, which have largely replaced personal savings.

With huge amount of money under their control, these funds exert tremendous pressure on business firms to perform and increase return on equity. There are only a few ways for firms to increase their profits. A time-honored practice during boom time is to raise capital and expand productive capacity. But the process takes time and involves great efforts while financial transactions are much easier and can be executed instantaneously. In short, the easiest way to increase return-on-equity is through leverage, and the best place is in the financial sector.

Institutional Setup, Social Attitudes and Power

For significant societal change to take place, it is not enough to have the appropriate institutional setup. This point is well brought out by countries with democratic institutions but with feudal values and social attitudes. The result is that people get far less than what they deserve.

Institutions cannot operate in a social vacuum. In other words, they operate in concrete societal contexts and are therefore affected by values, social attitudes, and concrete historical circumstances. But having institutions in place and supportive attitudes prevailing in society are still not enough, we need to have skillful people embodying the social attitudes to occupy the key positions to do the job. In short, we need a combination of institutions, social attitudes, and the right people in powerful positions.

Institutions, prevalent social attitudes in line with the values underpinning the institutions, and skillful social actors holding such attitude in key positions can combine to effect deep and far reaching consequences in society. We see this in the light regulatory institutional setups of American financial systems, prevalent neoliberal ideas and Mr Alan Greenspan and his team in position of power and influence.

The deregulation of the US financial system which began in the late 1950s to early 1960s was more or less completed in the late 1980s. In the UK, the most significant change was the Big Bang deregulation of the financial sector in 1986, sweeping away the traditions of centuries and turning the City of London into, in style and substance, Wall Street of Europe. By the early 1990s, the regulatory system has largely disappeared. It is either abandoned through the formal repeal of laws or by means of getting around it with clever innovations exploiting the legal framework.

Greenspan, who epitomizes the laissez faire economic philosophy, was chairman of the US Federal Reserve Board from August 1987 until his retirement in January 2006. From that very strategic position, he and his team of like-minded central bankers implemented a consistently easy money policy that many see as a crucial factor in the current crisis. Though not many people come to his defense now, it is important to note that his supporters and admirers far outnumbered his detractors during his terms of office. He served four presidents — Messrs Reagan, Bush senior, Clinton and Bush junior. It says something about the consensual support he enjoyed from both the Republicans and the Democrats. This brings us back to the nature of the intellectual climate and social attitudes following the fall of the Berlin Wall.

The victory in the battle of economic and political systems gives the winner a big boost which it used to its advantage in the battle of ideas. The most subtle yet pernicious impact is in the realm of culture and social behavior.

Whereas Marx talked about class struggle as the locomotive of history, the neo-liberal free marketers praise self-interest as the motor of economic progress. Every man for himself and the sum total is well being for all. From here, we are a very small step to condoning selfish behavior. It is instructive to read the following passage:

> People who are told there is no need to apologize for selfish behaviour tend to behave selfishly. Perhaps Ivan Boesky[b] went too far in proclaiming that greed

---

[b]Ivan Frederick Boesky was the icon of Wall Street excesses in mid-1980s. He was on the cover of Time magazine of 1 December 1986. He is a predecessor of Bernard Madoff of today. He is an American businessman who was sentenced to three and a half years jail and fined $100 million for insider trading in Wall Street in the mid-1980s. Based on tips received from corporate insiders, he placed bets on corporate takeovers and made a fortune of over $200 million. Source: http://en.wikipedia.org/wiki/Ivan_Boesky [accessed on 14 September 2009].

was good — or so the courts though[t] when they sent him to jail — but he captured the spirit of an age. Senior executives justify their large salaries and generous stock options by reference to fairness and market forces: which mean no more than that everyone else is doing it. Thirty years ago, such behaviour was constrained by unwritten codes of behaviour, and corporate managers were no more expected to use their positions to help themselves to the money which passed through their hands than were judges or policemen. Thirty years ago, high levels of unemployment, or homeless people sleeping in the streets, were assumed to be politically unacceptable. Today these things are not only politically acceptable but politically accepted.[21]

The passage is not lifted out of the pamphlets of social activists, haters of globalization, or left-wing sociologists. It is from the writings of John Kay, a mainstream management scholar.[22]

Example of a New Zeitgeist: One Dimensional Organization

It is a sign that times are changing and we have a new zeitgeist to express the mood and culture. Business firms have morphed from being multi-dimensional organizations into one-dimensional organizations.

Business firms perform several functions in society. They are supplier of useful products and services. They provide jobs for the working population, keeping them usefully busy. The workplace is for the employees a kind of community, where they socialize, learn, acquire a sense of identify and dignity. These features of employment are just as important as a source of income. Management of innovative firm wants the employees to enjoy working with the firm while making a contribution to the firm and society, and you see this idea being practiced in forward-looking and innovative firms like Nokia and Google.[23] In other words, business firms perform useful social roles as units of society, create value for the economy and enrich the lives of their employees. However, under immense pressure to "perform," business firms have atrophied to become more and more like money printing machines. The *stakeholder* view of business firms has given way to the *shareholder* view. Business school professors tend to embrace the idea that the only responsibility of business is to maximize profits. They have taught their students that as managers, their sole mission should be increasing shareholder value.[24]

The problem is not with profitability as a necessary condition for running a business in a market economy. The problem lies with profitability as the main or exclusive criterion. What has turned out to be harmful is not the care taken to assure that companies are profitable, but the belief that if they are profitable, then everything else must be all right.[25] Profit is being equated with success. Nothing succeeds like success, and success generates its own justification. Profitable companies must have done something right and virtuous. High income earners must be fine and admirable people too; their ways are to be emulated by others. If it may be put rather strongly, profit has become religion and money has become god.

Writing in the early 1970s about the very successful British retailer Marks & Spencer, Peter Drucker (known as the guru of management gurus) asks in what way profit features as an objective in the retailer.[26]

> The answer is that there has never been one. Profit goals have been anathema at Marks & Spencer. Obviously the company is highly profitable and highly profit conscious. But it sees profit not as an objective but as a requirement of business, that is, not as a goal but as a need. Profit, in the Marks & Spencer view, is the *result* of doing things right rather than the purpose of business activity. It is, above all, determined by what is necessary to attain company objectives. Profitability is a measurement of how well the business discharges its functions in serving market and customer.

Being solely focused on profit maximization can lead a firm down the slippery slope of cooking the book, neglecting the central role of adding value to customers, forgetting its core business, and even resorting to reckless risk-taking. Indeed, strategically speaking, profit maximization by itself can lead to disaster and is self-defeating in the long haul.

Students, Patients and Citizens Become Customers

What is even more disturbing is that such zeitgeist has exerted a profound impact on non-business organizations. Business organization has become the model for other organizations. Non-business organizations like hospitals and universities, and even NGOs have adopted the modus operandi of the corporate world. Schools adopt the language of business management, with various mission statements splashed over the walls. Students, patients and citizens become customers; universities begin to advertise themselves just like cars and jeans in the mass media, websites and buses. It is a cultural shift in society where the language of business firms has crept into the running of non-business and non-profit organizations.

If a good business cannot and should not be measured by a single criterion of success, this applies all the more so to non-business organizations like schools and hospitals. It is true that there are some objectives that can be measured by quantitative indicators such as mortality, number of patients treated or examination scores. However, organizations have other attributes that cannot be simply captured by numbers. Indeed, quantitative indicators would tend to limit or even distort their social goals.

Market was seen not only as the primary mechanism of producing economic wealth but was also being gradually accepted as the primary means of delivering public goods. As the political philosopher Michael Sandel puts it, "... we have to think through the moral limits of markets. We need to recognize that there are some things that money can't buy and other things that money can buy but shouldn't. Looking back over three decades of market triumphalism, the most fateful change was not an increase in the incidence of greed. It was the expansion of markets and of market values into spheres of life traditionally governed by non-market norms. We've seen, for example, the proliferation of for-profit schools, hospitals and prisons; the outsourcing of war to private military contractors. We've seen the eclipse of public police forces by private security firms, especially in the US and the UK where the number of private guards is more than twice the number of public police officers. Or consider the aggressive marketing of prescription drugs to consumers in the United States. [...] without quite realizing it, without ever deciding to do so, we drifted from having a market economy to being a market society."[27]

Such addiction to market displays a lack of understanding of the evolution of market economy. This was pointed out years ago by Karl Polanyi[28] and recently by Amartya Sen:[29]

> All affluent countries in the world ... have, for quite some time now, depended partly on transactions and other payments that occur largely outside markets. These include unemployment benefits, public pensions, other features of social security, and the provision of education, health care, and a variety of other services distributed through nonmarket arrangements. The economic entitlements connected with such services are not based on private ownership and property rights.
>
> Also, the market economy has depended for its own working not only on maximizing profits but also on many other activities, such as maintaining public security and supplying public services — some of which have taken people well beyond an economy driven only by profit. The creditable performance of the so-called capitalist system, when things moved forward, drew on a combination of

institutions — publicly funded education, medical care, and mass transportation are just a few of many — that went much beyond relying only on a profit-maximizing market economy and on personal entitlements confined to private ownership.

Even though Adam Smith explained the positive contributions of market capitalism, he was aware of the huge limitations of relying entirely on the market economy and profit motive. "Indeed, early advocates of the use of markets, including Smith, did not take the pure market mechanism to be a freestanding performer of excellence, nor did they take the profit motive to be all that is needed."[30]

Social Costs

The laissez faire economic system is supposed to be both efficient and fair. Compared to the planned economy of the Soviet Union, it is certainly more efficient. But is it fair? Let us look at the following facts about income disparity, healthcare and imprisonment as indicators of social conditions.

Income Disparities

The period since the late 1980s has seen a steady increase in profits and stock prices. This should be sound business and economic reason for companies to reward their workers for their contributions and to provide them with job security. In the face of changes in social attitudes, and pressures from the capital market, they have chosen not to do so.[31]

Wealth disparity in the USA and Britain reached levels not seen since the 1920s. The gains from recent economic growth flowed disproportionately to the wealthy. According to one study by Robert Gordon of Northwestern University and Ian Dew-Becker of Harvard, the top 10 percent of earners received the lion share of the benefits of the "productivity miracle" of 1996–2005. Another international study revealed that only Mexico and Russia had more unequal income distributions than the USA.[32]

The ascent of neoliberal thinking in the USA produced a departure from previous trend of low social disparity. Consider the real income of American families during the 58-year stretch from 1947 to 2005. During the first half of the period from 1947 to 1976, the economy delivered dramatic improvements in the standard of living of most Americans: median real income more than doubled. In contrast, during the period from 1976 to 2005, median real income registered an increase of 23 percent.[33]

Healthcare

Health statistics also tell another aspect of the story. The gap between the life expectancy of the top 10 percent and the bottom 10 percent was 2.8 years in 1980; that gap increased to 4.5 in 2000.[34]

Within the rich world, people in countries with lower Gini coefficient live longer, have lower rates of obesity, delinquency, depression and teenage pregnancy than those in countries with higher Gini coefficient.[35]

In 2005, only 14 percent of American workers were union members, compared with 27 percent in 1979. The decline may also help to explain the political acceptance of low tax and low regulation regime. Political parties are no longer as dependent as before on union donations. A study in the late 1990s of congressional elections of the US found that 81 percent of political donation givers earned more than $100,000 a year and only 5 percent earned less than $50,000.[36]

Prison Conditions

America seems addicted to using its prison system to solve its social problems, even though the results have not been encouraging. America has less than 5 percent of the world's people but almost 25 percent of its prisoners. It imprisons 756 people per 100,000 residents, a rate nearly five times the world average. About one in every 31 adults is either in prison or on parole. Black men have a one-in-three chance of being imprisoned at some point in their lives.[37]

Prison conditions do not speak in Uncle Sam's favor either. More than 20 percent of inmates report that they have been sexually assaulted by guards or fellow inmates. Federal prisons are operating at more than 130 percent of capacity. One-sixth of prisoners suffer from mental illness of one sort or another. There are four times as many mentally ill people in prison as in mental hospitals.

As well as being brutal, prisons are ineffective. They may keep offenders off the streets, but they fail to discourage them from offending. Two-thirds of ex-prisoners are re-arrested within three years of being released. The punishment extends to prisoners' families, too. America has 1.7m "prison orphans" and they are six times more likely than their peers to end up in prison themselves. The punishment is also not limited to imprisonment. America is one of the few countries that bar prisoners from voting, and in some states that ban is lifelong: 2 percent of American adults and 14 percent of black men are disenfranchised because of criminal convictions. It is indeed sad to know that this is the practice of a great nation founded on the ideals and principles of the European Enlightenment.

Looking at the USA, one is often reminded by an observation of the Belgian statistician Adolphe Quetelet: "Society prepares the crime, and the guilty person is only the instrument."[38]

The war on drugs also contributes its fair share. The number of people locked up for drugs abuse has increased from 41,000 in 1980 to 500,000 in 2009, or 55 percent of the population of federal prisons and 21 percent of those in state prisons. An astonishing three-quarters of prisoners locked up on drug-related charges are black.[39]

Just like in the USA, all is not well in Great Britain as a result of the wave of deregulation and laissez faire economy. "British society polarized: the relative prosperity of the new 'enterprise culture' was matched by the decay of inner cities and their despairing underclass, by falling standards in education, and by juvenile crime."[40]

One can argue that it is too simplistic to associate the above social problems with the ascent of market fundamentalism. However, one needs only to compare the social conditions among the rich countries which run market economy. The Nordic countries, Germany, the Low Countries and Japan have retained a significant role of the state in social welfare and their citizens have suffered less social ills than their counterparts in the

USA. In the case of Great Britain, the sad story of shift can be found in the pages of John Kay.[41]

Moral Values in Economic Life

One good thing the crisis has brought to the world is that political leaders are openly acknowledging the role of moral values in economic life. Speaking to the European Parliament in March 2009, British Prime Minister Gordon Brown suggested that the moral contagion that has afflicted market economies ran counter to a common European belief that "liberty, economic progress and social justice advance together, or not at all." Europe, he went on to say, had learned the truth that "riches are of value only when they enrich not just some communities, but all." He added: "As we have discovered to our cost, the problem of unbridled free markets in an unsupervised marketplace is that they can reduce all relationships to transactions, all motivations to self-interest, all sense of value to consumer choice and all sense of worth to a price tag."[42]

In a way, it is strange as well as refreshing to listen to Mr Gordon Brown. On his watch as the British chancellor of exchequer, the City of London enjoyed the "light touch" regulation and American banks and investment houses flocked to build up their London operations. He appeared to have accepted a Faustian deal under which the unbridled excesses of the City were tolerated because they generated windfall tax revenues for the Labour government to splurge on public sector spending.[43]

Writing in the September 2009 issue of the monthly Japanese journal *Voice* just before the general election,

Yukio Hatoyama, head of the Democratic Party of Japan and the current prime minister, says:[44]

> In the post-Cold War period, Japan has been continually buffeted by the winds of market fundamentalism in a US-led movement that is more usually called globalization. In the fundamentalist pursuit of capitalism people are treated not as an end but as a means. Consequently, human dignity is lost.
>
> How can we put an end to unrestrained market fundamentalism and financial capitalism, that are void of morals or moderation, in order to protect the finances and livelihoods of our citizens? That is the issue we are now facing.
>
> In these times, we must return to the idea of fraternity — as in the French slogan "*liberté, égalité, fraternité*" — as a force for moderating the danger inherent within freedom. Fraternity as I mean it can be described as a principle that aims to adjust to the excesses of the current globalized brand of capitalism and accommodate the local economic practices that have been fostered through our traditions. [...] Under the principle of fraternity, we would not implement policies that leave areas relating to human lives and safety — such as agriculture, the environment and medicine — to the mercy of globalism.
>
> Our responsibility as politicians is to refocus our attention on those non-economic values that have been thrown aside by the march of globalism. We must work on policies that regenerate the ties that bring people together, that take greater account of

nature and the environment, that rebuild welfare and medical systems, that provide better education and child-rearing support, and that address wealth disparities....

Endnotes

1. Paul Krugman (2007). Who was Milton Friedman? *The New York Review of Books*, 54(2).
2. *Ibid*
3. Franklin Allen and Douglas Gale (2007). *Understanding Financial Crisis*. Oxford: Oxford University Press; Gary Dymski and Robert Pollin (1994). *New Perspectives in Monetary Macroeconomics: Explorations in the Tradition of Hyman P. Minsky*. Ann Arbor: University of Michigan Press; Alan Greenspan (2007). *The Age of Turbulence*, New York: The Penguin Press.
4. Bill Bradley, Niall Ferguson, Paul Krugman, Nourie Roubini, George Soros, Robin Wells (2009). The crisis and how to deal with it. New York Review of Books, 56(10); Paul Krugman (2009). *The Return of Depression Economics and the Crisis of 2008*. New York: WW Norton.
5. The Four Little Dragons refer to Hong Kong, Singapore, South Korea, and Taiwan. The Tigers refer to Indonesia, Malaysia and Thailand.
6. Jawaharlal Nehru (1934–35). *Glimpses of World History*. Republished in 2004. New Delhi: Penguin.
7. Alan Greenspan (2007), pp. 130–131.
8. Walls seem to carry deep symbolic meaning. The Great Wall is a cultural symbol of China and there are Great

Wall restaurants and shops all over the world. Even the word *Wall* has powerful symbolic attribute, as in Wall Street.

9. Willaim D Nordhaus (2004). The story of a bubble. *The New York Review of Books*, 51(1);
   JM Roberts (1996). *A History of Europe*. Oxford: Helicon.

10. Alan Greenspan (2007). p. 12.

11. George Soros and Judy Woodruff (2008). The financial crisis: An interview with George Soros, *The New York Review of Books*, 15 May 2008.

12. John F. Burns and Landon Thomas Jr (2009). Anglo-American Capitalism on trial. *The New York Times*, 28 March 2009. http://www.nytimes.com/2009/03/29/weekinreview/29burns.html [accessed on 1 June 2009].

13. The original quote is: "Next to a battle lost, the greatest misery is a battle gained." Angela Partington, (ed.) (1992). The Oxford Dictionary of Quotation, 4th Ed. Oxford: Oxford University Press.

14. Robert Guest (2009). Red tape and scissors. *The Economist*, 30 May 2009.

15. Willaim D Nordhaus (2004).

16. Paul Krugman (2007).

17. *Ibid*

18. Alan Greenspan (2007).

19. Bo Zhiyue and Chen Gang (2009). Financial crisis enhances stand of China's New Left. *EAI Bulletin*, 11(1).

20. Robert Skidelsky (2001). The world on a string. *The New York Review of Books*, 48(4).

21. John Kay (1996). *The Business of Economics*. Oxford: Oxford University Press, p. 147. p. 138.

22. He contributes columns to *The Financial Times*, radio and TV broadcasts, is Visiting Professor of London School of

Economics, and the director of several public companies, and has been advisor and consultant to both parliamentary select committees and governments.

23. John Roberts (2004). *The Modern Firms*. Oxford: Oxford University Press.
    David Vise and Mark Malseed (2005). The Google Story. New York: Delacorte Press.

24. Foreswearing greed, *The Economist*, 6 June 2009.

25. Charles Hampden-Turner and Alfons Trompenaars (1993). *The Seven Cultures of Capitalism*. New York: Doubleday, p. 44.

26. Peter Drucker (1973). *Management: Tasks, Responsibilities, Practices*. New York: Harper Business, pp. 98–99.

27. Michael J Sandel (2009). *Justice: What's the Right Thing to Do?* Farrar, Straus and Giroux;
    Michael J Sandel (2009). 2009 BBC Reith Lectures — A New Citizenship http://www.bbc.co.uk/programmes/b00729d9 [accessed on 20 August 2009].

28. Karl Polanyi (1975). *The Great Transformation*. New York: Octagon Books.

29. Amartya Sen (2009). Capitalism Beyond the Crisis. *New York Review of Books*. Volume 56 number 5.

30. *Ibid*

31. John Kay (1996).

32. Philip Coggan (2009). Easier for a camel. *The Economist*, 4 April 2009.

33. Noam Chomsky (2009). Crisis and hope — Theirs and ours. *Boston Review*, September/October http://bostonreview. net/BR34.5/chomsky.php [accessed on 28 August 2009]; Paul Krugman (2007).

34. Philip Coggan (2009). More or less equal? *The Economist*, 4 April 2009.

35. Always with us? *The Economist*, 28 February 2009.
    Gini coefficient is a measure of income disparity. The higher the Gini coefficient, the greater the disparity.
36. Philip Coggan (2009). More or less equal? *The Economist*, 4 April 2009.
37. A nation of jailbirds, *The Economist*, 4 April 2009.
38. Always with us? *The Economist*, 28 February 2009.
39. A nation of jailbirds, *The Economist*, 4 April 2009.
40. Norman Davies (1996). *Europe*. Oxford: Oxford University Press p. 1075.
41. John Kay (1996).
42. John F Burns and Landon Thomas Jr (2009).
43. John F Burns and Landon Thomas Jr (2009).
44. Yukio Hatoyama (2009). A new path for Japan, *The New York Times*, 26 August 2009. http://www.nytimes.com/2009/08/27/opinion/27iht-edhatoyama.html [accessed on 9 September 2009].

Chapter Three

A Tale of Two Crises

Worldly wisdom teaches us that it is better for reputation
to fail conventionally than to succeed unconventionally.

John M Keynes[1]

The previous chapter identified the fall of the Berlin Wall
as a defining moment in understanding the current economic crisis, and it may be added, the 1994 Mexico and
the 1997 Asian financial crises. While the demise of the
Berlin Wall marked the end of the Cold War, it heralded
the beginning of a new phase in global financial market,
with all its opportunities, challenges and pitfalls. The
Asian crisis persuaded the affected East Asian countries
to adopt a policy of saving massive piles of foreign
exchanges as a protective measure against currency
attacks by speculators. This, together with the savings of
the oil-rich exporter countries, is the so-called Asian saving gluts. The savings parked in the USA allows America
to enjoy a fabulous decade of good life — low interest
rates and consumption-driven economic growth.

As explanation for the increase of capital flow in the
1990s, one obvious important factor was the reduction in
various forms of capital controls in the emerging countries.

But this in itself was not a whole picture because a number of countries had an open door financial policy well before the 1990s. Indonesia, for example, had essentially an open capital market since 1970. The Berlin Wall story provides the missing piece of the puzzle.

The turbulence of the financial markets across Latin America and East Asia was deeply enmeshed in the societal changes in the rich western countries. It shows the connections of separate events across continents — how the ageing population in the West and lax financial supervision in Thailand could, together with other factors, collaborate to brew a nasty financial typhoon.

The financial turmoil of Mexico was touched off by the cross-border flight of portfolio capital. Though the trouble was soon over, it was followed by the bigger and more devastating Asian currency crisis. This was followed by the collapse of the Russian ruble in August 1998 and the devaluation of the Brazilian real on 3 January 1999. Other currencies in Africa, Asia and Latin America soon suffered the same fate. The contagion of the financial crises in Russia and Brazil is one of the causes of the Argentinian crisis of 2002. Sharp depreciation of Brazilian real in 1999 affected export from Argentina.

Perhaps the most valuable lesson from the two crises is that sound long-term economic fundamentals of a country are a poor safeguard against speculative attacks. The best example of this point is Hong Kong. It has huge foreign reserves, fiscal rectitude, sophisticated economy well-known for its free market and open economy. It should be one of the last places to stir the appetite of adventurous speculators. But stir it did and its currency was the target of a stream of concerted raids by international speculators.

Four Features of the New Capital Flow

One factor that appears in almost all the literature on the two crises is the flow of foreign capital in search of high returns in the emergent economies. The deluge of capital inflow began in 1990 even though the profit opportunities in East Asian economies were probably greater in the 1980s than in the 1990s.[2] This new capital flow exhibited four notable features.

1. Beginning in the early 1990s, capital rushed into emerging markets in unprecedented quantities. By, mid-1990s developing countries were receiving 40 percent of global foreign direct investment (compared with 15 percent in 1990) and accounted for 30 percent of global portfolio equity flows (compared with 2 percent at the start of the decade).[3] The amount of capital inflows tripled between 1987–1989 and 1995–1997, to a total of more than $150 billion a year in the latter period.[4]

    Asia was the main destination of the deluge. The most fundamental change in the majority of East Asian economies in the 1990s was the dramatic increase in inflows of international capital. In 1996 alone, total net capital flows amounted to $110 billion compared to an annual average of under $17 billion a decade earlier.[5] The same year saw a new inflow of $93 billion of private capital to Indonesia, Korea, Malaysia, the Philippines and Thailand.[6]

2. The nature of financial markets also underwent a crucial change since early 1990s. In the mid-1980s official capital flows to less-developed economies exceeded private capital flows. A decade later, private flows were more than seven times the volume of official flows.[7] During the 1984–1989 period, net private capital flows and net official capital flows to developing countries average $12.5 billion and $26.5 billion per year respectively. Since 1989, there is a radical change in the nature of such capital flows. The corresponding figures for the 1990–1996 period are $141.7 billion and $27.4 respectively. In 1996, net private capital flows were $214.8 billion and net official capital flows were $2.4 billion.[8] It has been described as a change from a government-led international monetary system to a market-led international monetary system.[9]

3. Private funds flow into emerging economies either as foreign direct investments or as short-term bank loans, investments in stock market and real estates. The latter category has a short time horizon. They behave like hedge funds, mutual funds, or investment funds. At the first sign of trouble as perceived by them, they rush for the door. In the process, they inadvertently or otherwise contribute to a panic which cascades into a market crash. Private sector actors, especially those in short term capital movements, are not bearing their shares of the costs that crises generate. The investment horizon of fund managers is short term because they are judged on their quarter-to-quarter (or month-to-month) performance.[10] Their investment behaves very differently from monies from

governments and global institutions like the World Bank. When these official institutions lend money to the emerging economies, they lend it for a long time.

They therefore act as valuable shock absorbers, especially in times of financial stress. When the loans turn sour, they are willing to take years to hammer together a plan to restructure the loan.

4. Loans pouring into the emerging markets are the end result of a new financial engineering process of securitization. As a result of the process, tens of thousands of mutual funds and bond holders have replaced bank syndicates as the dominant source of private finance to developing countries. This presents special difficulties in debt work-out arrangements in the event of crisis. The number of such groups of creditors is too large to identify and organize. Moreover, governments have little influence over them. The situation is easier to handle for non-securitized debts. There is an international system for debt work-outs for sovereign creditors through Paris Club, and for bank creditors through the London club. The systems have worked pretty well, because the number of creditors has been small.[11]

The volume and pattern of capital flows explain a striking development in the 1990s. It is that financial crises in emerging markets can undermine the stability of the global financial system.[12] This view is expressed by the then US Treasury Secretary Robert Rubin. He says in an interview, "I can't imagine that twenty or twenty-five years ago my predecessors would have been worried about an economic crisis in Thailand or Indonesia or even

Korea."[13] This observation is well illustrated by the Mexican peso crisis and the Asian financial crisis. Both crises have attracted a substantial body of literature.[14,15]

The Mexico Crisis of 1994

After a decade of stagnation and high inflation, the Mexican government introduced a series of reforms in 1985 and economic stabilization plan in 1987. The results were resumption of economic growth, with an average of 3.1 percent per year between 1989 and 1994. As its economic reforms made steady progress, foreign investors began to flock to the country. The money flow was helped by the absence of control of capital inflow. "Indeed, large capital inflows began in 1990, when a successful foreign-debt renegotiation was formalized."[16] With a rosy economic outlook, several factors combine to bring about a sharp expansion of credit: a substantial drop in public debt, a huge amount of international securitized debts, a boom in stock market and real estate. From December 1988 to November 1994, credit from local commercial banks to the private sector rose in real terms by 277 percent, or 25 percent per year. Credit card liabilities rose at a rate of 31 percent per year, direct credit for consumer durables rose at a yearly rate of 67 percent, and mortgage loans at an annual rate of 47 percent, all in real terms. The total external financial flows to the private sector were also huge: $97 billion over the 1989–1994 period. A substantial portion of the increase in private investment went into unprofitable ventures. During the three years prior to the crisis, international investors had poured $45 billion into Mexican money market.[17]

In retrospect, we can see that the use of a predetermined exchange rate to deal with inflation, a large capital influx and a weak banking system would lead to exchange rate overvaluation, a vulnerable financial system and eventually a currency crisis.[18] And there was a frenzy of public spending before the presidential election, short term loans from foreign banks. Trouble began in the second quarter of 1994 when US real interest rates rose sharply, which was translated into problem in servicing loans.

The economic difficulty was compounded by events on the political front. The year 1994 began with an armed rebellion breaking out in the state of Chiapas. In March, the presidential candidate of the ruling Partido Revolucionario Institucional (PRI), Luis Donaldo Colosio, was assassinated, and this was followed by the assassination of the secretary-general of PRI in September. These events were interpreted as evidence of political instability and investors began to withdraw their funds. The government defended the currency by buying peso until it was clear that it was running out of foreign reserves.

On 20 December 1994, the Mexico government under new president Ernesto Zedillo devalued the peso against the American dollar by 15 percent, half of what economists had been suggesting. Speculators expected more devaluations to come and rushed to dump pesos and Mexican stocks and bonds. The peso suffered a free fall and by early 1995 it had declined 40 percent against the dollar. In the end, the Mexican government had to float the peso. The crisis spread to other emerging economies in Latin American, East Europe and Asia. It exercised a highly destabilizing and contagious effect on the international financial system. It took decisive and quick action initiated by Washington to stop the runaway markets before they dragged the world economy down with them — $49.8 billion in loans and guarantees for Mexico from the US and its allies. The *BusinessWeek* (13 February 1995) makes this comment: "Certainly, this will go down as the largest socialization of market risk in international history."[19]

Mexico bounced back rapidly from its banking crisis in 1994 and indeed registered a significant output gain relative to pre-crisis trend. Compared with most other countries hit by banking crisis, Mexico had much stronger export growth following its crisis.[20]

The very quick recovery suggests that though Mexico did make some mistakes, they were not serious enough to warrant such severe sufferings. Indeed, the Argentine-American economist Guillermo Calvo asked a very relevant question: "Why was so large a punishment imposed for so small a crime"? Only a few days before the crisis, the IMF had predicted an upswing of the Mexican economy. Until December 1994, Mexico was hailed as the prime example of market-oriented reform. "There was debate over the bloated current account deficits and overvalued real exchange rate, and the need for some corrections prior to the 'ascension', but the strength of the country's fundamentals was rarely questioned."[21]

The observation of Paul Krugman is worth reading[22]:

In the aftermath of the tequila crisis it was too easy to revisit the policies followed by Mexico in the run-up to the crisis, and find them full of error. But the fact was that at the time they seemed pretty good, and even after the fact it was hard to find any missteps large enough to justify the economic catastrophe of 1995. We should have taken Calvo's question — with its implications that there were mechanisms transforming minor policy mistakes into major economic disasters — to heart. We should have looked more closely at the arguments of some commentators that there really were no serious mistakes at all, except for the brief series of fumbles that got Mexico on the wrong side of market perceptions and set in motion a process of self-justifying panic.

The crisis was described by the then head of the IMF Michel Camdessus as the first financial crisis of the 21st century. Perhaps, it is more correct to call it the first post-Cold War financial crisis. Given that the end of the Cold War marks a watershed in the both the quantity and quality of private capital flows into emerging economies, the Mexico crisis may be seen as the first serious international financial crisis triggered off by the new wave of cross-border flight of portfolio capital.

Before the crisis, Mexican economic performance was pretty impressive. Its long term fundamentals were good, if not excellent. Unlike the past, there was no fiscal profligacy, hyperinflation and lack of export competitiveness. Thus, the outbreak of the crisis caught many analysts and observers by surprise.[23] Perhaps even greater surprise greeted them when Asian financial crisis broke out in 1997. Like Mexico, the emerging economies in East Asia liberalized their financial markets. With free flow of capital, both corporate firms and banks took advantage of the low interests in the USA, Japan and

Europe and borrowed hungrily from the banks there. But the ASEAN economies before the outbreak of the crisis were in much better shape than Mexico.

The Asian Crisis of 1997

The crisis first appeared in July 1997 in Thailand and soon spread to the rest of ASEAN countries, South Korea, Hong Kong and Taiwan. Viewing the Asian crisis retrospectively, some may have a feeling of *déjà vu*. Institutional investors from the rich countries saw opportunities in these fast growing Asian economies to earn extra returns for their portfolios. With fixed or stable exchange rates, both the borrowers and lenders did not see any need to hedge their transactions. The loans supplemented local savings as the East Asian countries had high saving rates. High local saving rates and lots of foreign money led to a credit boom in the early and mid-1990s. As prime investment opportunities decreased the credit boom was directed more and more to real estate and stock market speculation as well as marginal industrial projects. As governments tried to cool the overheated economy with tighter monetary policy, assets prices began to head south. Problems appeared in the form of declining export, leading to trade deficits. The hike of US interest rates in the second quarter of 1994 hit those who borrowed in US currency very hard.

These problems were noticed by investors and speculators and hedge funds. They started to sell the local currency. Government tried to defend its currency by buying it in the foreign exchange market. It soon gave up when its foreign reserves dwindled. The collapse of one currency set off a panicky flight of capital from other countries that exhibited real or perceived similar financial fragility. The speculators turned their attention to other East Asian economies with similar problems, and attacked them. The result was massive depreciation of local currencies. Business firms and financial institutions with debts dominated in foreign currencies went bust. At the height of the crisis the Korean won fell by 50 percent of its value *vis-à-vis* the US dollar, and the Indonesian rupiah fell by 80 percent. In 1997, there was a net outflow of $12 billion from Indonesia, Korea, Malaysia, the Philippines and Thailand.

But it is always easy to construct a retrospective account of Asian financial disaster. A more relevant question is whether the pre-1997 situation of these countries represented weak medium or long term fundamentals of their economies. Were there hyperinflation or signs of it, huge fiscal deficits, deteriorating current account deficits, and other indicators of misguided macroeconomic policies? The answer is a clear "no."

Since the mid-1980s, these countries had been chalking up impressive growth. Hong Kong, South Korea, Singapore and Taiwan were known as the four Little Dragons while Indonesia, Malaysia, the Philippines and Thailand the four Asian Tigers. For a decade from 1985 to 1995, Thailand might justifiably be seen as the paragon of an emergent economy. With an average GDP growth of 9.8 percent per annum it was the fastest growing country in the world during the period. "This growth marked an increase of more than 3 percentage points over that registered in the earlier decade, 1975–1984, and was propelled by quantum jump in domestic investment ratio, from 28.2 percent in 1985 to 41.0 percent in 1995. The important point to note …is that …it was domestic rather than foreign saving which financed the major part [of] the growing capital accumulation."[24] Until 1996, the Thai economy showed signs of excellent health. Almost all the macroeconomic and social sector indices were above the general norms, suggesting very strong fundamentals of the Thai economy. Though there was the issue of current account deficits, export growth remained far in excess of GDP growth. Moreover, growing domestic savings were the main form of investment funding with foreign borrowings playing supplementary role. Indeed, it would be outlandish then to suggest that trouble was on the horizon.[25]

However, the country suffered a jump in current account deficits in 1995 and 1996.This led to doubts about its balance of payments and possible sharp depreciation of the local currency in the near future. Buttressing this perception was the stagnation of exports and the scale of non-performing loans of financial firms. Whether the perception is well founded or not is not relevant. The key issue is whether investors share this perception. If enough number of speculators believe that the answer is "yes", they will attack the currency. They may turn a minor economic hiccup into a devastating crisis. This train of events represents very briefly what Thailand encountered in the crucial months from May to July 1997. Encouraged by their success, the speculators turned their attention to other East Asian economies that bore some resemblance to Thailand's. Though the affected countries had much better economic fundamentals than Mexico, they suffered a worse fate than Mexico in terms of its severity and contagion. The crisis led to a long, deep and painful recession. In Indonesia, it degenerated into a political crisis which brought down the long-ruling Suharto regime.

The IMF was called upon to help in the fire fighting. Its first priority was to look after the interests of the creditors with bailout money. And as usual, it prescribed its standard formula of austerity and tight fiscal and monetary policies. Those countries which followed the prescriptions of the fire fighter were soon facing disastrous consequences in the form of plummeting foreign exchange and riots in the streets by those badly hurt by rising food prices. Reflecting on the performance of the Fund during the crisis, Alan Blinder, a Princeton professor of economics and former Vice Chairman of the US Federal Reserve makes the following observations[26]:

1. Austerity is not always the right medicine. Tight monetary and fiscal policies may be useful in situation of large budget deficits and high inflation, as in Latin America in the 1980s. But this situation does not apply to Asian countries in the Asian crisis.

2. Devote resources to protecting innocent bystanders. It is necessary to give greater weight to developing and strengthening the social safety nets to help the poor from the impact of financial crises. The IMF and the World Bank should ensure that foreign creditors are not bailed out first while local peoples suffer.

In the midst of the turmoil, the Malaysian Prime Minister Dr Mahathir Mohamed showed his independence of mind by defying the IMF. He imposed currency control and pegged the Malaysian ringgit to the dollar. His policy proved to work and won him kudos. He may thus be credited for demolishing one important plank of the IMF's favorite prescriptions.

Exploits of the Three Musketeers

The financial crisis of Mexico was resolved pretty quickly with the intervention of the Washington with the assistance of the IMF and a few other countries. This enhanced America's stature and intellectual authority not only in the region but also elsewhere. A few years on, during the Asian financial crisis, America again played a central role in trying to sort out the messy situation. The response to the Asian crisis of 1997–1998 was the reinforcement of the American model of financial capitalism, the so-called Washington Consensus.[27] That was the high point of this variant of free market capitalism, and it was celebrated in style with the publication of an issue of *Time* magazine on 15 February 1999. The cover carries the headline "The Committee to Save the World" and shows the photos of US treasury secretary Robert Rubin, Fed chairman Alan Greenspan and deputy treasury secretary Lawrence Summers. The cover also invites its readers to savor "the inside story of how the Three Musketeers have prevented a global economic meltdown — so far." Inside was a glowing story of how the three heroes of laissez faire economy had "forged a unique partnership to prevent the turmoil from engulfing the globe." They masterminded IMF rescue packages for the Asian economies in distress through weekend meetings and late night conference calls.[28] When it was clear that the crisis threatened US financial markets, Greenspan quickly lowered interest rates, notwithstanding his earlier fears about "irrational exuberance" in the stock market. He then followed it up with a second rate cut when the first was not enough.[29]

Washington might have believed that the Asians were mesmerized by the intellectual brilliance and sincerity of the Three Musketeers and the IMF. However, not all the East Asian countries were so persuaded. Hardly any Asian victim country has deepened its affection for Uncle Sam and the IMF. The Fund was seen by many in Asia (and perhaps in other parts of the world too) as the "front man" of Washington. During the meltdown and especially in the aftermath, the IMF came under a barrage of criticisms, which drew sympathetic agreement from some western scholars and even financiers like George Soros. They accused the IMF of applying double standards, and of acting more to protect the interests of western banks at the expense of the borrower countries. Worse still, the Fund imposed tight monetary and austerity fiscal policies that hurt the poor and the innocent victims of the crisis. Some see the crisis as an opportunity for the USA to strengthen the grip of its hegemonic power. "With the end of Communism, the Asian tigers were seen in Washington as competitors, increasingly independent of US tutelage, hence the need to re-subordinate them ... The IMF entry means the return of US hegemony and the decline of Asian capitalism as an independent and competitive pole."[30] It has been noted that "the US government took advantage of the crisis to push long-sought trade goals."[31]

Geopolitical Dimension of the Crises

After the fall of the Berlin Wall, the US assumes the unrivalled leadership role not only in the strategic, but also in the economic and ideological spheres. This point is clearly brought out in the Mexican peso crisis and even more so in the Asian financial crisis.[32]

It is salutory to note the different approaches adopted by the USA with regards to the two crises. The White House acted promptly and decisively to contain the Mexican crisis and helped the economy on track again. It is certainly not an act inspired by altruism. Uncle Sam obviously did not like the idea of a flood of workers and farmers made destitute by the crisis streaming across the border. The victim countries of Asian countries could not enjoy similar American attention because they would not pose the same problem. There is also the factor of the geopolitics after the fall of the Berlin War.[33]

> Moreover, in the post-Cold War era, the US is less indulgent towards its allies because they are no longer needed to contain a Soviet Union that had collapsed... US economic interests have increased in relative importance to security concerns and it was prepared to take advantage of the crisis in order to seek greater deregulation and market penetration into East Asian markets for US corporate interests. If the crisis had erupted during the height of the Cold War, it would have undermined the appeal of capitalism and perhaps pushed certain impoverished masses to embrace revolutionary movements. In the context of Cold War rivalry, it would probably have been unlikely for the US not to actively assist the frontline states of

South Korea located on a divided peninsula, Thailand situated next to the Indochina war zone, and Indonesia which had experienced an abortive communist coup.

But in the aftermath of the Cold War, the US has less security imperatives to assist South Korea, Thailand and Indonesia; it prioritizes its economic interests. Not only did the US not push for debt rescheduling, it even torpedoed Japan's attempt to establish an Asian Monetary Fund to assist the crisis-stricken Asian economies.

Like many Asian economists, George Soros sees the policies that the IMF advocated before that crisis as having helped to cause it by going too far in insisting on the liberalization of capital markets, i.e., in encouraging countries to accept long-term and short-term loans without effective controls on their possibly damaging effects (for example when capital is suddenly withdrawn by a foreign creditor). With his usual bluntness, Soros points out that "the IMF was even proposing to include the opening of capital markets among its core objectives at the time the Asian crisis erupted."[34]

While the crisis had damaged the image of the IMF, it was good for China in the following ways.[35] First, the crisis, together with the floods in the summer of 1998, gave the Beijing government an alibi for the slowdown of the economy which had begun before the crisis. Second, Beijing's decision not to devalue the *renminbi* helped Hong Kong to hold on to its fixed exchange rate with US dollar. Its prompt action to rescue Hong Kong from raids by hedge funds speculators endeared it to the business community and local people there. Third, China declared its determination to the world that it would not devalue its currency. Though devaluation would boost its exports, it would also fuel inflation at home. The decision was welcome all over the world. It subsequently took the initiative to negotiate free trade agreements with the ASEAN countries. In retrospect, the crisis has turned out to be a milestone in its relationship with ASEAN and stimulated regional integration in East Asia.

Economic Fundamentals versus Speculative Capital

The Mexican crisis and the Asian crisis were preceded by large inflows of foreign capital over a number of years. What apparently triggered the crisis was a sudden jump in the current account deficit to GDP ratio which had remained at a fairly steady level over a number of years. However, this sudden change did not imply a weakening of economic fundamentals. To the speculators, even purely transient change could be perceived as a sign of an imminent serious problem in balance of payment. If a sufficient number of speculators shared such perception, it could induce a massive attack on the currency, thereby making the expectation self-fulfilling.[36]

The Mexican and the East Asian experiences suggest that strong economic fundamentals cannot be an effective defense against the onslaught of a currency crisis. "What matters is the perception of investors who may be guided by fundamentals, purely short term exchange rate expectation, or simply by how fellow investors are behaving, the implication being that economic fundamentals can lead to a currency crisis, only if investors have realized their past mistakes and revised their reading of the fundamentals."[37]

Indeed, Thailand was in a much better state than Mexico in terms of economic performance and macro-economic policies. Capital inflow into Thailand was used largely for investment, not consumption. Inflow was accompanied with commensurate increase in investment ratio. Deployment of capital was much more efficient. It had high savings; it was supplementing domestic savings with foreign capital to augment her productive capacity, and not as a substitute as in the case of Mexico. GDP growth was much more export oriented. The Asian melt-down has prompted economists to reconsider the merits of free capital flow, the role of the IMF and ways to protect themselves against vagaries of the global financial market.

Asian Foreign Reserves

A particularly prominent role in spreading boom and bust is filled by capital movements that increasingly build up and are then suddenly cut off.[38] It is a valuable insight distilled by Charles Kindleberger in his classic study of financial history of Western Europe. In the light of the two crises, this insight acquires extra significance. The Asian countries have learned through their bitter experiences the lesson that capital inflow ought to be treated with caution. There was a lively debate on the kind of strategy to deal with speculative attacks. Some called for long-term restrictions on international capital flows, and not just temporary controls in times of crisis. "The crisis demonstrated that even in countries that had balanced rapid growth with macroeconomic stability, reliance on mobile foreign capital, particularly short-term loans, entailed major risks."[39] Moreover, they have had bad experiences with the IMF.

The debate produced a strategy of building up large foreign reserves in order to stave off future crises.[40] They would keep their currencies stable to promote export-led growth and become net *exporters* of capital. Whether acting in concert or otherwise, the Asian economies have decided to build up a credible war chest, far in excess of the need to cover short-term imports. They would use their export earnings to accumulate large cushions of foreign-exchange reserves, most of them in dollars. As a result of this macroeconomic policy which was developed from the 1997 crisis, America was able to become what a *Financial Times* columnist calls the "borrower and spender of last resort."[41]

It is certainly not an ideal policy. Their purchase of US Treasury securities earned them meager interests while their business firms must pay much more for borrowing in dollars. The policy carries an opportunity cost of nearly one percent of GDP, according to Dani Rodrik of Harvard University.[42] At the same time, it helps to prop up the dollar, denying America the use of a cheaper dollar to stimulate its exports, and more exports will reduce its current account deficits. Moreover, it allows Uncle Sam to live beyond his means, which is certainly not in his long-term interest. In short, it is bad for everybody. The world is in need of fresh ideas to craft a win-win arrangement.

Special Lesson

Perhaps the most valuable lesson from the Mexican and the Asian crises is a new phenomenon brought about by free flow of capital. In such environment, strong long term fundamentals of a nation's economy are a poor safeguard against speculative attack against a currency with pegged exchange rate. It may endure indefinitely in the absence of a speculative attack. However, it may collapse if the currency is subjected to a massive and concerted attack.[43] The success of the attack depends on whether it is carried out by a large number of traders. Because of the uncertainty of the outcome, we need to look at the factors that encourage the traders to act as if they were guided by an invisible co-coordinator. Traders are influenced by others' behavior, thinking that these players have reliable information — a phenomenon known as herd behavior. This herd behavior is exhibited in making loans to borrowers as well as withdrawing loans. "As happened in Thailand and other Asian countries in 1996, foreign investors fall over themselves to lend money to countries they know little about because everyone else is lending money to them."[44]

Information uncertainty and herd behavior pose serious threat to fixed exchange rates regime in a global market of free flowing capital. "When fund managers can deploy their resources in a large number of markets across the world, their incentive to collect detailed, country-specific information is considerably weakened. Lacking any firm basis for forming expectations, investors then tend to attach undue weights to gossip and rumors. No less important is the fact that fund managers are generally judged on the basis of their performance in relation to that of others."[45] The danger of speculative attack is enhanced when traders can draw upon credit lines very swiftly and cheaply, which is possible in a global money market powered by advanced IT systems. "This has made pegged exchange rates highly vulnerable. In the absence of any significant transactions costs and problems of arranging credit, it pays a trader to take a position against the currency if there is some probability of a crisis: in case the crisis materializes, the trader gains; but he does not suffer even if the peg endures."[46]

Endnotes

1. John Maynard Keynes (1936). *The General Theory of Employment, Interest and Money*, New York: Prometheus Books, p. 158.
2. Stephen Grenville (2000). *Capital Flows and Crisis*. In Noble and Ravenhill, p. 40.
3. World Bank (1997). *Private Capital Flows to Developing Countries: The Road to Financial Integration*. Oxford: Oxford University Press.
4. Gregory Noble and John Ravenhill (2000). *Causes and Consequences of the Asian Financial Crisis*. In Noble and Ravenhill, p. 3.
5. *Ibid.*
6. Cheol Eun and Bruce Resnick (2009). *International Financial Management*, 5th Ed. New York: McGraw Hill.
7. Gregory Noble and John Ravenhill (2000). *Causes and Consequences of the Asian Financial Crisis*. In Noble and Ravenhill, p. 3.
8. Mihir Rakshit (2002). *The East Asian Currency Crisis*. New Delhi: Oxford University Press.

9. Tommaso Padoa-Schioppa and Fabrizio Saccomanni (1994). Managing a market led global financial system, in *Managing the World Economy: Fifty Years after Bretton Woods*, Peter Kenen (ed.), Washington DC: Institute for International Economics.

10. Stephen Grenville (2000), p. 51.

11. Lawrence Summers (1995). Ten lessons to learn, *The Economist,* 23 December 1995.

12. Bong-Chan Kho, Dong Lee and Rene M Stulz (2000). US Banks, crisis, and bailouts: From Mexico to LCTM, *Working Paper 7529,* National Bureau of Economic Research, Cambridge, MA.

13. Thomas L Friedman (1999). *The Lexus and the Olive Tree.* New York: Farrar Strauss Giroux, p. 186.

14. For the Mexico crisis, consult the following for example: Thomas W Slover (1998) Tequila Sunrise: *Mexico Emerges from the Darkness of Financial Crisis*. London: London Institute of International Banking, Finance and Development Law.

   US General Accounting Office (1996). *Mexico's Financial Crisis: Origins, Awareness, Assistance, and Initial Efforts to Recover.* http://www.gao.gov/archive/1996/gg96056.pdf.

   Nora Lustig Mexico in crisis, the US to the rescue: The financial assistance packages of 1982 and 1995 (Brookings discussion papers).

   G A Calvo and E C G Mendonza (1996). Petty crime and cruel punishment: Lessons from the Mexico debacle. *American Economic Review, Proceedings of the American Economic Association*, 86(2).

   Francisco Gil-Diaz (1998). The origin of Mexico's 1994 financial crisis. *The Cato Journal*, 17(3).

15. For the Asian Crisis, see, for example, the following books:
    Karl D Jackson. (1999) (ed.) *Asian Contagion.* Oxford: Westview Press.
    William Hunter, George Kaufman and Thomas Kreuger, (ed.) (1999). *The Asian Financial Crisis*, Boston: Kluwer.
    Woo, W T, J D Sachs, and K Schwab (eds.) (2000). *The Asian Financial Crisis: Lessons for a Resilient Asia.* Cambridge, MA: MIT Press.
    Gregory Noble and John Ravenhill (eds.) (2000). *The Asian Financial Crisis and the Architecture of Global Finance.* Cambridge: Cambridge University Press.
    Gerald Tan (2000). *The Asian Currency Crisis.* Singapore: Times Academic Press.
    Mihir Rakshit (2002). *The East Asian Currency Crisis.* New Delhi: Oxford University Press.
16. Francisco Gil-Diaz (1998). The origin of Mexico's 1994 financial crisis. *The Cato Journal*, 17(3).
17. Cheol Eun and Bruce Resnick (2009).
18. Sebastian Edwards (1996). A tale of two crises: Chile and Mexico. *Working Paper 5794*, National Bureau of Economic Research, Cambridge, MA.
19. Quoted in Cheol Eun and Bruce Resnick (2009).
20. M Ayhan Kose, Guy Meredith, and Christopher Towe (2004). How has NAFTA affected the Mexican economy? Review and Evidence. *IMF Working Paper 04/59* Washington: International Monetary Fund.
21. GA Calvo and ECG Mendonza (1996). Petty crime and cruel punishment: Lessons from the Mexican debacle, *American Economic Review, Proceedings of the American Economic Association,* 86(2), quoted in Mihir Rakshit (2002), p. 66.

22. Paul Krugman (2009). *The Return of Depression Economics and the Crisis of 2008*. New York: WW Norton, pp. 53–54.

23. Sebastian Edwards (1996). A tale of two crises: Chile and Mexico, *working paper 5794*, National Bureau of Economic Research, Cambridge, MA.
    Mihir Rakshit (2002). The East Asian currency crisis, New Delhi: Oxford University Press.

24. Mihir Rakshit (2002), p. 44.

25. *Ibid.*

26. Alan S. Blinder (1999). Eight Steps to a New Financial Order, *Foreign Affairs*, 78(5), pp. 50–63.

27. Harold James (2009). The making of a mess, *Foreign Affairs,* 88(1), pp. 162–168.
    George Soros (2002). *On Globalization* Public Affairs.

28. Time magazine, Rubin, Greenspan & Summers Feb 15, 1999. http://www.time.com/time/covers/0,16641,19990215, 00.html.

29. Roger Alcaly (1999). He Has Got the Whole World in His Hands, *The New York Review of Books*, 46(15).

30. Quoted in Paul Burkett and Martin Hart-Landsberg, East Asia and the crisis of development theory, *Journal of Contemporary Asia,* 28, p. 451.

31. Gregory W Noble and John Revenhill (2000). *Causes and consequences of the Asian Financial Crisis*. In Gregory W Noble and John Ravenhill (2000), p. 22.

32. Paul Dibb, David Hale and Peter Prince (1998). The strategic implications of Asia's economic crisis. *Survival,* 40(2).
    Robert Zoellick (1998). The political and security implications of the East Asian crisis, National Bureau of Asian Research, *NBR Analysis,* 9(4).

33. Lam Peng Er (2000). The Asian financial crisis and its impact on regional order: Opening Pandora's box. *The Journal of Pacific Asia,* 6, 57–80.

34. George Soros (2002). On Globalization Public Affairs.

35. Wang Hongying (2000). Dangers and opportunities: the implications of the Asian financial crisis for China. In Gregory W Noble and John Ravenhill (2000).

36. Mihir Rakshit (2002), p. 52.

37. *Ibid*, p. 73.

38. Charles Kindleberger (1993). *A Financial History of Western Europe*. 2nd Ed. Oxford: Oxford University Press, p. 268.

39. Gregory Noble and John Ravenhill (2000), p. 32.

40. Paul Krugman (2008). What to do. *The New York Review of Books,* 55(20).

41. Robert Skidelsky (2009). The World Finance Crisis & the American Mission, The New York Review of Books, 16 July 56(12).

42. Not even a cat to rescue. *The Economist* online edition, 20 April 2006.

43. Mihir Rakshit (2002).

44. Robert Skidelsky (2001) The world on a string, *The New York Review of Books*, 48(4), 8 March.

45. Mihir Rakshit (2002), p. 27.

46. *Ibid*, pp. 27–28.

Chapter Four

Insights from Japan's "Lost Decade"[a]

Introduction

In retrospect, the most dramatic turning point in the half-century of Japan's postwar economic development was the collapse of the property and stock market in 1990. The collapse ushered in a very long period of recession known as the "lost decade".[1] Japanese economy experienced average annual real growth of 0.8% from 1991 to 2001.[2] One would expect that with fiscal stimuli, the economy would recover as in a normal business cycle. But somehow the recovery simply refused to show up. Conventional wisdom of economic stimulation does not tally with the Japanese experience of the long recession. The "lost decade" has acquired such an iconic status that economists and business columnists have evoked it as a possible prospect of the current recession for the USA.[3]

---

[a]An excerpt of the chapter appears in October–November 2009 issue of *Today's Manager*, a Singapore management magazine. A slightly shorter version of the chapter is published as a working paper of East Asian Institute. National University of Singapore.

Indeed, as the second largest economy in the world and operating in an electoral democratic framework, its experiences may shed some light on the nature of recession of an advanced industrial economy in the context of globalization, as well as the limitations of monetary and fiscal stimuli to deal with such a recession.

There are three reasons for us to study Japan's experiences for insights. First, America's and the UK's troubles are in some deep sense similar to Japan's. They are a result of a real estate bubble and easy credit. The prices of resident property in 10 largest cities of the USA doubled in five years, just like those prices in Japan's big cities during the bubble period.[4] What is more disturbing is that nationwide, prices of resident units, and commercial property in the US and the UK shot up more than they did in Japan. It is also relevant for Asia because a property bubble preceded the 1997 crisis. Second, Japan shares the essential features of an advanced industrial economy with Western Europe and the USA. The "lost decade" is likely to hold lessons for them. Third, the Japanese trajectory of economic development has offered very useful concepts for other Asian countries to emulate. This pattern is captured metaphorically in the "Flying Geese" model.[5] The Japanese developmental state model emphasizes the troika (ruling party, bureaucracy, and business); other Asian countries on their own designed generally a state-led developmental model before the Flying Geese model was articulated.

Contrary to popular perception formed by press reports and research works, zombie banks and slowness in cleaning them up are not the main reason for the long recession. The suggestion of increasing domestic demand as the solution also needs careful examination. The market crash has produced an economic situation that failed to respond to the combined attack of fiscal and monetary stimuli. It is also a case of liquidity trap. It is argued that Japan's problems are those of an advanced industrialized economy confronted with an over-sized bubble bursting. The aftermath of the bubble is a balance sheet recession that has been basically cleared after more than a decade. To move ahead, Japan has to embark on a program of innovation to increase productivity and value-adding activities. At the same time, Japan has an ageing population *and* a very restrictive immigration policy. This is a serious issue that demands solution at the level of ideas and culture.

Brilliance before Bubble

The magic of Japanese economic miracle for half a century lies in a simple yet crucial fact. It was able to produce goods in high demand in a global economic order that favors free trade. Japan in the 1950s was well known for its cheap plastic toys. In the 1960s, its light Honda motorbikes appeared in big numbers in towns and cities in Asia. It manufactured small and fuel efficient cars, and against the backdrop of 1973 and 1979 oil crises, they had special appeal. Not surprisingly, the cars were enthusiastically endorsed by taxi drivers in many countries. And by the 1980s, "made-in-Japan" conjured up images of consumer electronics of the highest quality. In the second half of the 1980s, Japan had above-trend growth and very low inflation, and Japanese banks were considered among the strongest in the world.[6]

Between 1950 and 1973, the Japanese economy doubled in size every seven years, and it had achieved one of the highest standards of living in the world.[7] In the four decades prior to the bubble in 1990, Japan stole the show in economic development. It had the world's highest saving rates and displayed an endless and amazing capacity to adapt to the latest industrial technology. Japanese manufacturing became legendary. It coped pretty well with the inflationary spurt in the wake of the OPEC oil price hikes in 1973. After the 1970s, the technological strengths of Japan's machinery and other manufacturing industries continued to prop up the economy, using exports as a lever. This strength was based on the innovative capacity of its technological firms.[8] They entered and successfully competed in high-tech terrains, which were previously the preserve of US and European multinationals. Their prowess measured in terms of patents and productivity was the result of systematic and continuous investment in Research and Development (R&D). A study of the US Academy of Engineering published in 1987 observed that Japan was superior to the USA in 25 of 34 critical technologies.[9] To make the story more complete, we must also mention that Japan spent much less of its taxpayers' money on defence compared to other rich countries and could therefore single-mindedly pump the money into promoting economic growth. For that it had to be grateful to America as its closest ally who provided the defence umbrella.[10]

The 1970s and 1980s were the brilliant decades of Japan when the Japanese economy attracted much fear and admiration. As the economy expanded, the R&D expenditure steadily increased. Japanese firms were able to apply the results of their R&D efforts to make products much in demand. Moreover, the firms were able to produce more patent applications per R&D dollar spent than their US counterparts. The star performance has spurred many studies and inspired the appearance of books such as *Japan as Number One* by Ezra Vogel in 1979 and *The Enigma of Japanese Power* by Karel van Wolferen in 1989.

Background to the "Lost Decade"

As the US economy gained steam in 1983–1985 and the dollar surged in value, US import from Japan rose dramatically. Japan was under pressure to reduce its trade surplus with the US by appreciating the yen exchange rates. As a result of the Plaza Accord in September 1985 and subsequent central bank intervention and market forces, the Japanese yen rose rapidly. The result was a shock to the Japanese economy and the high yen "slump."[1] To halt further yen appreciation, Japanese monetary policy shifted toward a more expansionary stance. Between 1985 and 1987, the Bank of Japan discount rate was cut from 5% to 2.5%, and it remained at this level through 1989. At the same time, Japan embarked on a program of financial liberalization, partly in response to pressure for more open competitive markets. The move stimulated price competition among financial firms and prompted them to take greater risks.[12]

The combination of financial liberalization and monetary expansion is generally blamed for creating asset price inflation in the second half of the 1980s. To cope with a mild slowdown in economic and employment growth, the government poured huge sums to stimulate the economy, most of them in public works projects, and ran up large budget deficits.[13] At the same time, financial liberalization had allowed major manufacturing firms to bypass banks in raising investment funds, and banks had consequently lost some of their best business. They responded by turning their attention to real estate and stock market. First stock and then land prices rose dramatically after 1986, more or less doubling in value over several years. The rapid rise in wealth-stimulated consumption spending helped to close a large portion of the trade surplus by the end of the decade. At the peak of its bull market, the value of land in Tokyo exceeded that of the state of California, and the total value of land in Japan was four times that of the USA.[14] It is useful to bear in mind here that the area of California is bigger than the area of Japan. This gives us an idea of the size of the bubble.

In the period of euphoria, the quality of debt deteriorates.[15] The low quality and over extended loan portfolios left Japanese financial and non-financial firms exposed to considerable risk. When monetary policy was tightened in 1989 and 1990, stock and land prices quickly shed most of their gains of the previous four years.

The collapse of the stock market and property market was not surprising. What was surprising was that the recession dragged on for so long in spite of massive prime pumping. For example, between 1992 and 1995, there were five fiscal stimulus packages, totaling ¥54 trillion.[16] As a result of the series of fiscal stimuli, Japan's public debt is huge. It was ¥836 trillion at the end of June 2007, according to the Ministry of Finance.

Its public-debt ratio stood at 65 percent of GDP in 1990, ballooned to 175.5% in 2006 and to about 180% in 2009.[17] Even after a series of fiscal stimuli, there was no sustainable recovery.

Many Japanese firms and banks entered the 1990s with a heavy debt burden left over from the bubble years. Some banks went under and a number of them merged. Many manufacturing firms had substantial excess capacity after the investment boom of the 1980s. It takes time for the firms to pay back the loans and to work away the excess production capacity. These are two clear attributes of a weak economy. Fixing the financial system cannot be achieved simply by continuously pumping cash into the commercial banks. Japanese banks have been often advised that they must get off the life support system, restructure themselves so that they earn decent profits and function normally again. This is only partly correct. Banks are financial intermediaries. They cannot function effectively as banks when households and business firms have to clean up their debts before they dare to borrow money.

Two Approaches to Get Japan Out of Recession

Conventional wisdom prescribes the aggressive use of fiscal and monetary expansions to stave off a recession. Based on its successful track record in dealing with recession in many countries over several decades, Keynesian economics argues that insufficient demand is the cause of the recession. Except for the chaotic period just after World War II, Japan's postwar recessions are caused by a shortage of demand. Immediately after the War, the GNP dropped sharply to half that of the pre-war peak because imports from overseas had been cut off, which means that raw materials needed for productive activities were not available. This problem does not obtain now. The demand side arguments seem to hold true not only for Japan but also for other industrialized countries. However, after a series of expansionary fiscal actions, solid recovery simply refuses to come. Why have all the stimuli failed to pull the economy out of the deep valley of recession? This calls into question the effectiveness of such policies and therefore also the idea of a lack of demand as the culprit.

As the recession of the 1990s dragged on, the supply-side arguments had gained wide acceptance. The arguments attribute the long stagnation to the ageing population, rigid regulation, out-dated business models, and old production machineries. Between them, they have resulted in substantial reduction of the growth potential of Japan. This is the position taken by, for example, the *Economic Survey of Japan* published by the Economic Planning Agency in 1998. The white paper makes the following policy recommendation:

> To appeal for positive actions by all economic entities and revive the potential growth rate, Japan must urgently implement reforms to effect a transition to a market-mechanism and free-competition based economic and enterprise system with equality of opportunity, self-responsibility, information disclosure, and fixed rules as the main principles.

In terms of practical measure, it means liberalization, skill upgrading, more women in work force, and new machineries. Under Prime Minister Junichiro Koizumi, it went further by introducing privatization, i.e. the kind of policies used by Reagan and Thatcher two decades earlier.

Somehow these two approaches, even when combined, have not yielded the remarkable performance of the golden decades. Why?

The Liquidity Trap

Economics textbooks tell us that monetary authority can stimulate the economy by increasing the liquidity available in the financial system by lowering interest rates. The aim is to increase borrowing and lending, consumption, and investment. This policy has proved to work in many cases of economic downturn. However, there are situations when this policy fails to work even when the interest rate has been progressively lowered nearly to or equal to zero. Such a situation is known as a liquidity trap. It can lead to deflation that encourages people to postpone spending because they expect prices to drop further. This can only make a recession even more severe. Until the "lost decade," no country with monetary and fiscal stimuli has experienced liquidity trap and it was seen as just a theoretical possibility after the Deep Depression. Japan has shown to the world that liquidity trap can happen with such double barreled stimuli, and it is now joined by the USA.

In practice, why does this happen? Traditionally, the monetary authority increases the overall quantity of money available to the economy by injecting it into the real economy via banks. Liquidity trap occurs when banks are unwilling to lend, so the newly created liquidity is trapped behind unwilling lenders. It can also occur when businesses and consumers are not willing to borrow because they have to work away their debts accumulated during the boom years. Any further increase in the money supply along this path is not possible, as the nominal interest rate cannot drop below zero.

Various Explanations of Japanese Woes

Various reasons have been offered to explain the lost decade: ageing population, zombie banks, over-sized bubble, inadequate domestic demand, outmoded business models, too much regulation, rising labor cost, and competition from newly industrialized countries.

Ageing Population

A factor that appears repeatedly in discussion on Japan's future is its ageing population. Japan's population started to decline in 2005, by 0.02 percent per year, as did its labor force. The birth rate has dropped to less than 1.3 per woman (the replacement rate is 2.1). Life expectancy is the highest in the world. The eight-million baby-boomer generation of 1947–1949 is going to retire soon. By 2015, more than 25 percent of its people will be 65 years old or older. By 2025, the figure will be 30 percent compared to 12 percent in 1990. The proportion of working population, aged between 15 and 64 years old, is declining, from nearly 70 percent in 1990 to 65 percent in 2008 and is expected to decline to 60 percent in 2020.[18]

The ageing population has far-reaching impact on the technological future of Japan. In 2007, 18.2 percent of its workforce was engaged in the manufacturing sector. The figure was one of the highest among the G7 countries. If there is no large influx of young migrant workers into this sector, the unrelenting pressure of demographic change will in due course melt away Japan's technological foundation.[19] This is extra worrying because manufacturing remains the most productive sector of the economy and main earner of foreign exchange.

The issue of migration is an issue that needs to be solved at the cultural level. Given the nature of Japanese politics, the solution has to reflect the broad consensus of the people, and a radical change is not unlikely in the near term.

Too Slow in Cleaning Up Its Banks

Another common reason cited is that Japan was too tardy in cleaning up the mess in the banking sector. Even though the financial crisis affected the banks very badly, it was not until 1998 that Japan began to remove dud assets and recapitalize its banks. Because of the important role of banks in credit-driven economy, it is of utmost importance to restore the functioning of the banking system, almost akin to removing the blood clog in a patient's arteries. In practice, it means bold and swift action to clean up bust banks, recapitalize weak ones, and, when necessary, nationalize them. But the case of Japan is different from those countries that could adopt such line of action. It faced the additional complication that such a clean-up would require a large-scale restructuring of firms, and this in turn would cause mass unemployment.[20]

The Ministry of Finance failed to tackle the problem of non-performing loans (NPLs) aggressively, and this had grave repercussions as macroeconomic policy mistakes sank the economy into prolonged recession and exacerbated the magnitude of bad bank loans. The collapse of the bubble-saddled Japanese banks with enormous amount of NPLs. In the wake of the financial meltdown, the appropriate actions to take were aggressive disposal of bad loans, heightened prudential regulation, aggressive macroeconomic stimuli, or accelerated financial system reform. Bad loans disposal would help to restore bank capital ratios and thereby decreased the possibility of systemic risk triggered by bank collapse.[21]

For most part of the 1990s, the size of bad loans was not much worse than those in other countries that experienced banking crisis.[22]

Why is the banking problem so persistently seen as the main culprit for prolonging the recession? The explanation enjoys such currency because it sounds so sensible, rational, and reasonable. Moreover, it is a distillation of the Western experiences in dealing with their own crises.

But what about the case of Japan? Can the received wisdom really stand up to empirical examination? Richard Koo, the chief economist of Noruma Research Institute, answers the question in the negative, based on the following empirical evidences.[23] If banks had been the bottleneck, then we should have observed some phenomena typical of credit crunches. First, companies would turn to the corporate bond market for funding, but this did not happen. Second, foreign banks in Japan were not burdened with bad loans. They were in a position to lend to corporate borrowers but there was no significant increase in their lending activities. Third, many small-and-medium-sized companies and unlisted companies depend on banks for their funding. If there are few willing lenders but many willing borrowers, the latter would react to the situation by offering to pay higher interest rates. "But nothing remotely like this happened in Japan," writes Koo.[24]

Haphazard Policies

After several years of fiscal expansion had failed to revive the growth rate to a self-sustaining 3 percent growth rate, critical voices became loud enough to get notice. The subsequent debate became heated and resulted in an oscillating policy and a major policy blunder in 1997. After enjoying 3.6 percent growth in 1996, the Hashimoto government made a mistake with the April 1997 consumption tax increase from 3 percent to 5 percent, the end of special income tax cut and an increase in health charges. The matter was aggravated by the outbreak of the Asian financial crisis in Thailand three months later. The crisis hit Japanese banks too, especially those that had made loans to the affected countries. The crisis weighed down the already low consumer confidence and domestic demand just as the country was showing signs of recovery.[25]

Some strongly believed that had the massive fiscal expansion continued unabated, it could have helped to lift the economy out of recession. By rising demand, the cycle of rising bankruptcies could be reversed. However, this was not persistently tried, as only one third of the earmarked stimulus packages of 1992–1997 were actually undertaken.[26]

Another criticism was that infrastructure spending was disproportionately directed to rural areas instead of urban areas where the needs were greater and multiplier effects higher.

Overvalued Japanese Yen

As export has formed a powerful engine of economic growth, it is natural to train the search light at this corner. In 1971, the yen–dollar exchange rate was ¥360/$1, and it appreciated to ¥240/$1 in 1985 and it surged to ¥129/$1 in 1993.[27] The rate was ¥94/$1 in July 2009. The "ever higher yen" has been identified as one primary cause of the prolonged economic slump.[28]

Had an overvaluation of yen been the problem, then a fundamental solution to this problem is a continuous coordination between the Japanese and American monetary authorities toward achieving exchange rate stability.[29] It is believed that such an adjustable peg would provide the essential mechanism for Japan to break out of its economic woes.

However, the point of overvalued yen is not convincing because the appreciation of the yen in the late 1980s was simply a correction of the prior under-valuation. The long-term appreciation of the yen under the floating exchange rate system is more likely to be due to the higher labor productivity of Japan's export industries, mainly in consumer electronics, transportation equipment, precision machinery, general machinery, and manufactured metal products.[30] The US–Japan inflation rate differential plays no significant role. In fact, one could make the point that the bubble was partly due to the monetary easing that was wrongly introduced to curb the further rise of overvalued yen. More importantly, exports were extremely stable from the late 1980s through the 1990s, except for the temporary influence from the Asian financial crisis in 1997.[31] Whether the yen was strong or weak, Japan has enjoyed a current account surplus for almost all of the past decades.[32]

Weak Domestic Demand

At the end of the high-growth period in the 1970s:

> The Japanese economy failed to develop steady domestic demand. That is, domestic demand linked with improvements in the people's standard of living failed to rise, and this resulted in the excesses of the decade-long bubble. Healthy demand growth is dependent upon the right infrastructure, and this provides the answer to the pressing and practical question of what we should do now.[33]

Weak domestic demand forms a theme that appears very often in business press and scholarly discussion.[34] It is seen as the main factor that can resuscitate economic growth in Japan.

Against this argument, we can perhaps look at some figures collected by Hiroshi Yoshikawa of Tokyo University. Though he believes that the recession of the

1990s was caused by insufficient demand, he gives some figures that suggest another interpretation.[35] Between 1988 and 1993, the growth rate declined from 6.2 percent to 0.3 percent, a drop of 5.9 percent. During this period, the contribution of private investment to growth fell from 2.3 percent to –1.9 percent, a drop of 4.2 percent. Thus, fall in private investment accounted for some 70 percent of the overall decline. Similar relation is seen in the period from 1993 to 1996 when the growth rate rose from 0.3 percent to 5.1 percent, an increase of 4.8 percent. The contribution of private investment rose from –1.9 percent to 1.8 percent, an increase of 3.7 percent. During the second period, investment expansion accounted for nearly 80 percent of the increase of the growth rate. "Therefore, throughout the 1990s, capital investment was unquestionably the star in Japan's economic drama, accounting for the ups and downs in the nation's GDP growth rate."[36]

Another reason behind the low consumption can be found in the prolonged low interest rates. Interest incomes for individual savers have dropped by a trillion yen annually since 1995, and this formed a 2 percent drop in GDP and lower spending.[37]

The question of increasing domestic demand needs careful examination. Even in recession, Japan remains one of the richest countries in the world. The people enjoy high standard of living, and this is very convincingly manifested in their high life expectancy. Many in high growth countries who have to toil round the clock would be too pleased to trade places with the Japanese. Some termed it "Golden" recession since unemployment rate was quite low.

The rich are certainly able to spend more. But with general distrust of the long-run solvency of the state pension system, even they prefer to keep the money for future expenses. If people are not willing to spend, it is ethically wrong to force them to do so.

If rich Japanese feel that they have had a good life based on the current level of material consumption, why should they consume more? Moreover over-consumption by them can only increase the pressure on the environment.

Unlike the rich, the middle class cannot afford to spend because they have to save up for their old age. This is economic rationality that should be encouraged rather than discouraged. A better way is to increase the spending power of the lower social strata by increasing their wages. An OECD report says that the workers' share of GDP fell from a peak of 73 percent in 1999 to 65 percent in 2007.[38] Another is to subsidize childcare of the lower income groups, which has the additional benefit of promoting population growth. It shows here the close linkage between social policies and economic policies.

Some have suggested inflation targeting as a way to boost domestic consumption. This is not likely to work because households drew down their savings in an attempt to maintain the standards of living amid an ailing economy and falling incomes. As a result, household savings have been falling steadily.

> Households went above and beyond the call of duty to support the Japanese economy during this period, and were certainly not the cause of the long slump. That the household sector's financial surplus had fallen to

near zero between 2001 and 2004 suggests that households are already pushing themselves to the limit, and
cannot be expected to increase spending any further
unless incomes increase significantly.[39]

Over-Regulation

The manufacturing sector has demonstrated its ability to
compete in the global market based on its high productivity. It is the non-manufacturers that fared poorly. The poor-
est performers among this group are also the most heavily
regulated. They are in agriculture, construction, education,
healthcare, transportation, and communications.[40] Suffice
it here to look at two examples. The first example is the
construction industry where the procurement setup sustains highly inefficient and high-cost construction. An edi-
torial comment in the Japanese newspaper *Nihon Keizai
Shimbun* of 8 March 1999 reveals a lot[41]:

> Japan's public works budget is on the order of ¥34 tril-
> lion per year. This is equivalent to the sum total of all
> the public works ordered by the other leading indus-
> trialized nations combined. This makes Japan a con-
> struction giant of monstrous proportions. What is even
> more outrageous is that most of the works orders
> placed by local government bodies, which account for
> 70 percent of all public works, are knowingly given to
> local firms that have no construction capabilities
> whatever. These orders are then passed up to the lead-
> ing general contractors, just as they are. The local
> firms do nothing productive, but they pocket a tidy
> profit. Even under the current recession, there are still

a vast number of such highly profitable "paper" contractors, jostling about under the surface.

It must be added here that the construction industry is an important source of support for the long ruling Liberal Democratic Party (LDP).

Another example in the regulated sector is agriculture, another vote bank of the LDP. As a percentage of the GDP, this sector has been shrinking ever since the country embarked on a program of industrialization. In 1950, it accounted for 26 percent of the GDP and employed 46 percent of the workforce. By 1970, it produced 6.1 percent of the GDP and accounted for 18 percent of all employment. However, full-time farmers account for only a small proportion of the farming community and 1 percent of the workforce. The vast majority of farmers are actually salaried employees who happen to own land classified as agricultural land. By virtue of the geography, Japan's agriculture is not competitive. But the situation is aggravated by regulation. It is conservatively estimated that the profits gained when agricultural land is sold and converted to other uses are nearly 30 times the land's existing value. The prospects of reaping huge gains present problems for the true farmers, who are agricultural experts. They cannot pursue economy of scale because they cannot afford to buy extra land to enlarge their plots. Most other farmers have no interest in long-term investments to improve soil conditions.[42] The result is that Japan ends up with an inefficient agricultural sector. Japanese rice cost 10 times more than rice from Thailand. Japan's agriculture is seen as an impediment to genuine free trade agreement, which could have further boosted its GDP.[43]

The construction industry and agricultural sector provide clear examples of how electoral politics get in the way of economic rationality. The point here is not so much the existence of regulation as the wrong regulation. The issue is getting the regulation right, and designing and enforcing regulation that promotes economic growth and well-being of the people rather than pork barrel politics.

Outdated Business Models

The Japanese corporate networking or keiretsu provides an organization form for cross-shareholding within groups and ties between banks and the client firms.[44] It consists of a main bank, industrial enterprises and other financial firms. It was characterized by joint ventures among group firms, extensive intra-group procurement, and loosely integrated group decision making. They adopt the following as more or less standard practices: life-long employment, bonus payment, wages and promotion based on seniority, and enterprise unions.

Keiretsu, once lionized as a source of Japanese economic prowess, is now often cited as potential impediments to structural reform, especially with respect to introduction of market-based reform in corporate finance and governance. When viewed in positive light, keiretsu provides efficient solution to various market imperfections. It provides an intermediate or hybrid solution to the market and vertical integration dichotomy. It reduces problems associated with transaction costs through long-term relations without full vertical integration. This applies to product development, supply chain system management, insurance, and finance. The networking provides an organization mechanism for group members to share risk during financial distress. Core bank in a keiretsu plays a corporate governance role that is slowly being eroded because of more market mechanism.

Another element is the industrial policy under the direction of the Ministry of International Trade and Industry (MITI). It uses a range of methods — subsidized credits, assistance for collaborative research, preferential access to foreign exchange, and tax incentives — to advance the industrial policy by nurturing national champions to compete in the international market. Administrative guidance consists of a set of regulations implemented by the Ministry of Finance and MITI bureaucrats. But this industrial policy has been undergoing gradual and substantial change over the years.[45]

Shift to Low Productivity Sector

The biggest transition in the industrial structure during the high growth period was the shift from agriculture to manufacturing. In the period 1955–1960, the labor productivity in manufacturing was about 1.6 times that in agriculture. In leading manufacturing firms, the gap was in the order of six times. The end of the high growth period in the 1970s witnessed a change in the pattern. From 1970 to 1995, the GDP share of the manufacturing sector declined from 44.5 percent to 33.8 percent while that of the service sector increased from 49.4 percent to 64.4 percent. However, the labor productivity of the service sector is much lower than that of the manufacturing sector.

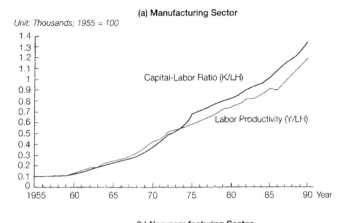

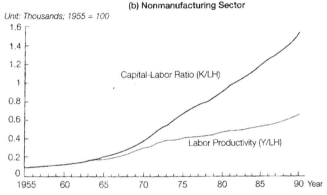

Capital-Labor Ratio and Labor Productivity (1955–1990)

Note: K = capital stock; Y = real GDP; L = number of employed workers; H = working hours.
Source Data: Economic Planning Agency, *National Accounts Annual* and *Private-Sector Enterprise Capital Stock Statistics*; Ministry of Labor, *Labor Statistics Monthly*.

Source: Japan Development Bank, *Surveys* (No. 171; May 1993); pp. 17–18.

From p.113 of Yoshikawa (2001) *Japan's Lost Decade*, Tokyo: The International House of Japan.

"This means that on the supply side, the Japanese economy has witnessed a long-term shift of production resources from high productivity to low productivity industries. In fact, this has been one of the main problems facing Japanese economy ever since the 1970s."[46] This mismatch between demand growth and productivity decline holds tremendous long-term consequences for the economy.

Changed Business Environment

It may be useful to recollect how Japan did so well before the onset of the crisis in 1990. The development of the Japanese economy is a combination of both the qualities of the Japanese people, and external environment and luck.[47] The high growth period coincided with a world-wide boom and expansion in world trade. It was able to invest in new technologies from abroad, import cheap raw materials, and export quality products. Japan was able to put in place supportive institutions at home. It had few competitors while operating in an expanding global market. During the Cold War period, the USA opened its huge market to its Japanese ally even though the latter was relatively protectionist.

But the environment has changed. The newly industrialized countries have already learned so well from Japan that they are churning out many if not all the goods that had once brought accolade to Japan. Though a good proportion of these goods are produced by Japanese companies relocated to China and Southeast Asia to take advantage of the low production cost, Japanese workers have lost their jobs and Japanese suppliers have lost their business. South Korea's Samsung and LG in televisions, China's Haier in home appliances, and Huawei and ZTE in data-communications threaten to do to Japan what Japan did to the USA and West Europe. They produce high-quality goods at lower prices.

Balance Sheet Recession

The most coherent and convincing explanation is one of balance sheet recession provided by Richard Koo.[48] In the late 1980s, Japanese firms were highly leveraged because their growth rates were high, and the assets they bought kept on appreciating. When the bubble burst, they discovered to their horror that their liabilities exceeded their assets. In other words, they were technically broke. Fortunately for them their core operations remained in good shape. Cash flow was robust, and the companies were generating good profits. Under such conditions, all the stakeholders would want the companies to continue operating. Declaring the companies bankrupt served no one. The managers and workers would be on the street, jobless. The shareholders would lose every cent of their investment. The creditors would get nothing back. The rational and responsible thing to do was to use the profit generated to pay back the loans as quickly as possible. No company under such conditions could be persuaded to take loans at zero interest. Because the hole on the balance sheet was so immense, it was not until the end of 2005 that net debt repayments had fallen to zero for the corporate sector as a whole. The good news: Japanese economic recovery is real.

Back to Basics

With the benefit of hindsight, one can see some of the roots of the current economic woes in the 1970s. In the aftermath of the oil price hike in 1973, Japan suffered a recession in 1974 and an inflation of more than 30 percent that year. Investment rates fell and growth slowed to the 5 percent range in the late 1970s. "This slowdown in economic growth was partly due to the lingering effects of the OPEC oil price shock, but more fundamentally it also reflected the rapidly diminishing returns to new investment as Japan converged with other developed market economies."[49] In other words, Japan began to experience the slower growth of a mature industrial economy. Meanwhile, the latecomers in the form of newly industrialized countries are fast catching up.

Traditionally, it was believed that land, labor, and capital are the important factors. Even if we are to broaden the factor of land to include natural resources and strategic geographical position, we still find this traditional concept inadequate. Suffice it to mention the often quoted cases of how some oil-rich countries have got stuck in their dependency on oil export as the main source of national income and fail to embark on the more arduous journey of industrialization.

The case of Japan provides a powerful argument for an alternative view, namely, the economic well-being of a country lies in its productivity, based on innovation broadly defined. One fruitful way of looking at innovation is offered by the economist Joseph Schumpeter.[50] He describes innovation as follows: (1) the introduction of new goods, (2) the introduction of new production methods, which may be based on scientific discovery, (3) the development of new markets, (4) the development of new sources of new materials, and (5) the creation of new organizational forms. He calls for new combinations of factors of production to replace old ways, as encapsulated in the famous concept of "creative destruction." In his framework, supply does not automatically create demand. One must be able to produce goods that are in high demand or have the potential to generate demand. Two examples of such goods today are cell phones and (especially for the young people) iPods but unfortunately they are not invented by Japanese firms. Another example is new drugs to enable senior citizens to stay healthy and continue to work. Japan is well positioned to embark on such innovation as it has a strong technological base and growing ageing population. Such medical and technological advances call for new scientific breakthroughs. "As they reached the technology frontier, Japanese firms have had to reorientate their R&D efforts from the application and refinement of existing, relatively well-developed technology to the creation of more fundamental breakthroughs."[51] The good news is that its electronics industry has shown continuing research productivity, in line with the trends of the 1980s and early 1990s. Even today, in spite of the long slump, Japan still has many world-class firms, most of them technological. For example, Toyota in car manufacturing, Nintendo in computer games, Shimano in bicycle parts, and Nikon in cameras and the precision lenses for making semiconductors.[52] But to break out of the economic doldrums, Japan needs many more of such companies. The world will be delighted if Japan can channel some of its restless innovative technological power to produce an array of green technologies.

Innovation can also take the form of enhancing the productivity of the service, agricultural, and other regulated sectors. Here a word of caution is in order. Rather than taking on the approach of business reengineering or process redesign once much in vogue in America, Japan will probably embark on the exercise on its own terms. Perhaps it is useful to be reminded that America is more an exception rather than a normal case in the world. Here Japan can take heart that the nation has an impressive track record in introducing reforms as illustrated by in its Meiji Restoration and its economic rejuvenation after World War II. Moreover, Japan provides a very fine example of how it has been able to place the welfare of the people and social harmony above attractive GDP figures.[53]

Schumpeter thus offers another way of looking at how Japan can seek a way out of the economic malaise. The dichotomy of supply and demand is not the right way to pose the question. In fact, it is a false dichotomy. Consider the case that manufacturers are so good in producing washing machines that there is an oversupply of them. It does not make sense for one household to have more than one washing machine. Fiscal and monetary expansion to stimulate demand does not solve the problem. Neither does a drop in wages as a means of cutting production cost.

On the business scene, a positive response to the economic challenge calls for entrepreneurs, i.e. business people with foresights and risk taking spirit (note: not speculation or gambling). Here there is much for Japan (and the rest of the world too) to learn from the business culture of Silicon Valley where risk-taking is an intrinsic part of lucrative adventures. It is therefore heartening to learn that the Tokyo government is trying to steer some of the business people from risk-averse culture where failure carries a stigma. It chartered an Association for the Study of Failure, which hoped to turn failure experience into knowledge at the society, corporation, and individual levels.[54]

At the same time, for an entrepreneur to be able to promote new combinations of factors of production, somebody must put the means of production in his hands. It is here that banks and credit can play an important role. The financial crisis that originated in Wall Street shows that Wall Street bankers have failed miserably in their duty as financial intermediaries.

To nurture creative and innovative minds, a special role has to be assigned to the education system. This point is paramount as Japan, being poor in natural resources, has to depend heavily on its human resources. The educational tradition in Japan emphasizes doing well in examinations, with good schools becoming experts in exam-drilling type of instruction, and with school and university students scoring top grades. The heavy load of books that students drag to school speaks volumes. Students are under immense pressure to perform in exam, and a few who cannot take the pressure prefer to take their own lives. For obvious reasons, students hate schools. The graduates of such system might have served the manufacturing and production activities brilliantly. But they could find it difficult to perform well in R&D activities. The challenge for Japan, and also for other members of the flying geese, is to make school a pleasant and enjoyable environment for discovery-based learning rather than exam focused learning. Students should be encouraged to reason for themselves. While they need to respect authorities, they must be encouraged to question authorities. All great truths begin as blasphemies, so says George Bernard Shaw.

The Relevance of Globalization

Globalization in its earlier form several decades ago has enabled Japan to pull off an economic miracle. It has continued to help Japan, which needs the rest of the world as sources of raw materials as well as market. However, of late, it has also posed a challenge to Japan in the form of the NICs. For example, Japan's laptop industry has been gradually losing ground to its Taiwanese counterpart. The way Japan runs its mobile telephony suggests that Japan is adopting a protectionist route. Its mobile technology differs from those used by most other countries.[55] By doing so, it loses a golden opportunity to carve for itself a strategic position in the global mobile phone market. None of the following recent and current big brands are Japanese: Ericsson, Motorola, Samsung, Nokia, and iPhone.

Given its creative and high-tech flair, Japan would do well to face up to the challenges of globalization, both for its own good and the good of others. Japan's growth will need to be driven by improving its productivity, investment abroad, and relocating some of its manufacturing activities overseas. Outward investment has helped Japanese firms maintain and even expand global market shares and contributed to the restructuring of the Japanese economy away from older industries. Given its huge current account surplus and programs of industrial development in many countries, Japanese outward FDI has scope for significant increase. The move is bound to affect low-level manufacturing at home. This will act as a catalyst in restructuring and upgrading of the Japanese economy toward more advanced activities with higher value added. Inward FDI is likely to have similar effect. Deregulation has opened up much of the industrial and service sectors to foreign participation, and in the process it has introduced new technologies and business practices. This has eroded the cross-shareholding relationship within the keiretsu groups, and has facilitated merger and acquisition activities between Japanese and foreign firms. The level of competition and inflow of foreign technology will increase, with higher productivity growth as a major result.[56]

The globalization perspective does not see stimulating domestic consumption as the magical solution to the economic problem. The argument for such "magical solution" assumes implicitly a linear model of social and economic development. Under such a model, something must be done to reverse the current trend of weak domestic consumption that results in anemic growth and growing trade surpluses. It must be noted that such linear model has proved to be wrong time and again in social change. Let us put aside such linear model and consider another approach to see how Japan can help itself and others by working out a better approach. Let us consider the world economy as an interlocking and mutually dependent system. Japan with its surplus capital and advanced technologies can play a positive role in exporting capital and technologies.

A special aspect of this is Japan's economic relation with China. After Deng Xiaoping's famous southern tour of the free trade zones, China embraced free market economy in greater scope and depth. Subsequent economic development has bound the fate of the economy of the two countries more tightly together. China's advance has hollowed out Japan's labor-intensive industries while it has provided Japan with a substantial market for high-quality consumer products and advanced technologies.

Japanese investment must not go around pumping money into areas where others can do well on their own. As long as it focuses on economically productive and socially useful investment, it will contribute to the growth and technological advancement of the host countries. There is a win–win situation for Japan to aim for. In the domestic scene, it focuses on making new technological breakthroughs, and improving its productivity and innovation in the service sector. Seen in this light, the trade imbalance is not a source of worry. Socially, Japan should be given the leeway to protect sectors that employ those who cannot catch up with the demands of such economic transformation. The good thing here is that unlike America, Japan has the deep tradition of placing society above economy.[57] Other countries would do well to refrain from exerting pressure on Japan and let it make its own decision. Social unrest in Japan is not good for its neighbors and allies.

Learning from Japan's Travails

We began this chapter by suggesting that the Japanese experiences could have something to offer in (1) understanding the problems besetting the USA and Britain,

(2) understanding the nature of recession in a mature economy, and (3) providing useful historical experiences for other Asian countries that are fast catching up in economic growth.

First, the Japanese experience holds a message for the USA and other countries that have suffered real estate bubble. In very bad cases, it leads to a long period of recession that fails to respond to aggressive monetary and fiscal stimuli. The price declines following bubbles can last for many years and excess capacity can take years to work off. Meanwhile owners of empty properties have to cough up money to maintain them. The fear that the USA may follow the footstep of Japan is real. However, a closer look suggests that things may not turn out so bad for Uncle Sam because of two reasons. The first reason lies in the fact that America is spreading the burden of its housing bubble across the whole globe. Foreigners hold a big chunk of American mortgage-based securities. Sovereign wealth funds have injected funds into American banks. Unlike the sharp appreciation of Japanese yen after the bubble burst, the American dollar has remained weak, which helps its export.[58] The other reason is demography. When the bubble burst in Japan, the country was already 10 years into decline of its working population, and the trend continues to this day. By contrast, America has continued to experience gradual population growth, which helps to work away the excess housing units. Having said this, the picture is still gloomy. Experiences of other countries of different backgrounds have shown that serious asset-price bubbles often lead to economic downturns lasting several years.[59]

Japan has entered the recession as a creditor nation rich in domestic savings. Its savings are estimated to be equivalent to $15 trillion. This is not the position enjoyed by the USA. In America, private sector debt shot up from $22 trillion in 2000 (equivalent to 222 percent of GDP) to $41 trillion in 2007 (equivalent to 294 percent of GDP). The corresponding figure in Japan was 35 percent. *The Economist* (14 February 2009) reports an estimate by Goldman Sachs, suggesting that American banks held some $5.7 trillion worth of troubled loans such as sub-prime mortgages and commercial property. This is equivalent to almost 40 percent of GDP.[60] The message is short but not pleasant. The USA and Britain may face a long and slow recovery and anemic growth for the coming years.

The second message suggests that we need to look at the limitations of fiscal and monetary stimuli, and at productivity as the fountain of economic well-being. In a mature economy with a high standard of living, such stimuli may fail to work their magic in a deep and painful recession. The social situation in the rich countries today is very much different from that in the 1930s and 1940s. Moreover, the world today does not present the USA with a huge export market, unlike World War II and the devastated landscape in its aftermath.

The key to economic well-being lies thus in productivity, innovation, and technological breakthroughs. The rich Western countries still boast of most of the top transnational companies, world-class research universities, and laboratories. Such resources should be tapped to become the core engines of economic growth. Instead of churning out consumer products whose supply has exceeded demand, it is in their enlightened interests to come up with green technological products and new ways of running businesses that release the creative potential of their employees. The whole world will welcome more of the types of Google, Apple, and Nokia rather than General Motors and Merrill Lynch. There is much for the world to learn from American dynamism and entrepreneurial spirit. After all, its IT industry has been the most dynamic sector of the US economy in the 1990s.

At the same time, there is much scope for increasing productivity. One simple way is to identify causes that increase costs unnecessarily, either directly in the cost structure of the company or via costs borne by society. Two examples of the first type are litigation and the patent system. The following report reveals how much can be saved in these two areas to boost the US economy.

Litigation cost the country $252 billion in 2007, according to Towers Perrin, a consultancy. At nearly 2 percent of GDP, that is about twice the burden that lawsuits impose on other rich countries. Yet the Pacific Research Institute (PRI), a conservative think-tank, thinks it a gross underestimate. By including indirect costs, such as products never launched for fear of litigation, PRI arrives at a total of $865 billion a year. Of this, it reckons two-thirds is wasted…

"Patent trolls" pose another problem. These are firms that buy up patents, not to turn them into products but solely to sue other firms that may have infringed them. Since the United States Patent Office grants patents freely and courts enforce them zealously, every inventive company lives in fear of trolls. If one can convince a court that a billion-dollar product incorporating hundreds of patents infringes only one of his, he can get an injunction to stop it being sold. The victim typically settles. Michael Heller, author of "The Gridlock Economy," argues that such vaguely defined and aggressively asserted property rights stifle innovation and cost lives.[61]

There are other areas that drain away American productivity. Suffice it to mention here healthcare, crime, high prison population, drug abuse, poor education, and traffic congestion. Though they are often featured in news reports and commentaries, they have a stealth-like quality. Their economic impact is often not too obvious to ordinary people. They are surely not problems that can be tackled easily or within the four walls of a firm. They are of a societal character and would require the political will, intellectual vigor, and cultural resources of the American society to solve them.

The third message is more relevant to the rest of the members of the flying geese. Financial liberalization is a process that can bring along some unexpected and nasty consequences. Certainly, it can be beneficial to some parties, but the overall result for the economy may be a long recession. Of all aspects of globalization, financial liberalization has a very vicious and poisonous tail. Malaysia did go along with financial liberalization, only to pull back during the Asian financial crisis. China and India have been very cautious in opening up their financial market and do not lift their control of capital flows. Events have vindicated the wisdom of their caution.

The Japanese experience tells us about the danger of relying on rising property or stock prices to produce nice GDP figures. There is a striking difference between the manufacturing sector and non-manufacturing sector in Japan. The latter invested heavily in real estate during the bubble period and created the bad debts that plagued the economy. Of course, banks that financed such speculation are also part of this sector. If they are lucky, they may reap huge profits, but that in itself will not and cannot enhance the competitive edge of the companies. In bad cases, it leads to the "lost decade" of Japan and the US subprime debacle. In milder cases, real estate speculation contributes to the cost of doing business by virtue of high rentals, and works against a country's global competitiveness. Moreover, capital channeled to real estate speculation means less money directed to productive investment. GDP growth built on rising property prices due to speculation does not produce real economic growth.

The next point is that in spite of the long recession, Japan has not experienced much social dislocation. Unlike other industrialized countries, Japan has been able to undergo drastic economic transformations without much social upheavals. This can be attributed, at least in large measure, to the primacy Japan has given to society above economy.[62]

Wider Societal Problems and Cultural-Intellectual Challenges

The main national concern of Japan after World War II has been to build a strong economy, perhaps in the hope that everything else will do well or will fall in place. The rising economy sustains a buoyant national spirit. When the economy gets stuck in a malaise, its mood turns blue. "The prolonged recession has given rise to a stifling feeling of being locked inside a box with no exit in sight, and has cast a dark shadow on the national psyche. The sudden increase in suicides as reported by Japanese newspapers is simply shocking."[63] It is not just shocking, it is also sad.

The recession is egregiously long and tenacious, which prompts deeper and more reflective enquiries. It is a crisis of governance in both government and business; a revival will require a fundamental overhaul of several institutions, though even reformers cannot agree among themselves as to what this means.[64] It is also a crisis that evokes the image of cul-de-sac. Policy makers in Japan recognize that the economic and financial arrangements that served Japan so well during most of the postwar period are no longer compatible with the new economic, technological, and political environments.[65]

Compared to other mature economies, Japan's unemployment rate should be considered normal. Crime rate is low. The situation of drug abuse can easily be the envy of America. In terms of societal indicators, Japan should be happy with itself. Here, one is reminded by the cliché that happiness is a state of the mind. It really is, if one has a roof over the head and food on the table.

Beyond the issue of economic growth, perhaps what Japan needs more is revival and rejuvenation in the field of culture, ideas, and intellectual exploration. Would not it be exciting to see many more of Japan's best and brightest being inspired to become poets, novelists, artists, essayists, men/women of letters, and philosophers who can express the spirit of the time in its loftiest forms and most forward-looking terms, to contribute something enduring to world civilization?[66]

Such cultural and ideational contributions have a pragmatic dimension too. They can provide a cultural and intellectual framework for social and economic reforms. The process of institutional change and reform involves all facets of society. Among other things, it depends on the ability of politicians, intellectuals, and managers to fashion an ideological consensus around distinct types of institutional change.[67] New institutions and institutional reforms need the cultural bedrock and progressive ideas associated with ground-breaking philosophies. For example, the narrow nationalism of Japanese is out of synch with the cosmopolitanism of the global condition. Such social and cultural attitude discourages immigration that is badly needed to cope with the problem of ageing population, a point we briefly touched on earlier.

Fall of LDP and Rise of DPJ

The "lost decade" is an important element in understanding the general election on 30 August 2009 in which the Democratic Party of Japan won a landslide victory. In throwing out the long-ruling Liberal Democratic Party the people have shown their disapproval of its continuing failure to respond to the fallout of the bubble. It is not really a vote on ideology since both parties are basically conservative.

During the election campaign, the DPJ appealed to the popular sentiment that under the LDP the people were losing a largely egalitarian society and a sense of economic security. Such certainties had been swept away by the reforms inspired by Anglo-American free market liberalism of former Prime Minister Junichiro Koizumi. In the campaign, the DPJ was given a hand by the global recession originating from Wall Street excesses. People were happy to lend their ears to DPJ leader Yukio Hatoyama's criticism of "unrestrained market fundamentalism and financial capitalism."

By early September 2009, the DPJ has pledged the following:

- To cut back big government construction projects. Some of the money saved will go to subsidies for green technologies, such as a proposal to pay half the cost of installing solar-power systems in homes. The new government wants to reduce Japan's carbon emissions by 25 percent below 1990 levels by 2020.
- To boost consumer spending by reducing taxes and fees. It plans to halve the petrol tax of ¥54 a liter and gradually eliminate highway tolls, reduce the tax rate for small firms from 18 percent to 11 percent, increase the minimum wage to ¥1,000 per hour eventually from ¥629, and roll back Koizumi's reforms that allow manufacturing firms to hire temporary employees.
- To improve health care, expand financial assistance for the unemployed and provide a minimum monthly pension of ¥70,000, give parents ¥26,000 a month for every child aged 15 and under, and remove the tuition fees for public high schools of around ¥120,000 a year.

Moreover, these measures are aimed at giving people a sense of financial security that hopefully has the side effect of encouraging them to spend more and boost domestic demand. If all goes well, the pro-family measures would nudge young couples to be "fruitful and multiply." Like many other socioeconomic plans or programs, there are some inherent inconsistencies, such as between its environmental policy and lowering petrol taxes. There is a huge question mark of how it is going to find the money to pay for the plans.

As to the ambitious carbon reduction goal, Hatoyama might well deserve the title of a visionary and not a dreamer. According to Martin Schulz of the Fujitsu Research Institute in Tokyo, the 25 percent target is not outrageously high, only just beyond what the European Union is pledging. The move is hailed by environmentalists, all the more so when Japan is already the most CO_2 efficient around. "We welcome the courage of Yukio Hatoyama and believe he has the strength to set Japan on track for a low carbon future which will benefit people and nature, both in Japan and worldwide."[68]

Conclusion

To achieve its goals, the DPJ need not depart radically from the way Japan is run. In other words, it does not need to dump the triangular relationship of the ruling party, the bureaucracy, and business. However, to broaden the social basis and resources of its program, it should welcome the participation of NGOs, social activists, and other groups of public-spirited individuals. Their inputs are all the more needed if the state is to encourage women to play the dual roles of mothers and members of the workforce. In the process of solving social-economic problems, a new institutional arrangement will evolve, open to input from more sources and more responsive to changing demands of an evolving global order. To paraphrase Putterman and Rueschemeyer, given Japan's role in global economy and the deep-rooted nature of its economic problems, the project represents historically an institutional innovation of the first order, based on tremendous political, economic, and cultural resources and guided by trial and error in the pursuit of large-scale enlightened interest.[69] It must eschew certain aspects of its protectionist tendencies and forge a forward-looking and cosmopolitan culture and undergo an intellectual rejuvenation to replace its narrow nationalism. To build a new model to take its place requires more than just political power. It needs fresh ideas and new cultures to underpin new mindsets and institutional innovations. In the process, it would contribute to the global economy and modern world civilization.

Endnotes

1. The term "lost decade" was used earlier when referring to the failures of development in the 1980s of many underdeveloped countries (as opposed to the First Development Decade in the 1960s and the Second Development Decade in 1970s). Also, with specific reference to the period 1990s, it has been variously described by scholars. While Yoshikawa refers to the 1990s as "Japan's lost decade," Joseph Stiglitz refers to the 1990s as "the roaring nineties: the greediest decade in world history." Other Asian countries experienced growth until the 1997 crisis, and the West experienced prosperity.

2. Fukao Mitsuhiro (2003). Financial Sector Profitability and Double Gearing, in Magnus Blomström *et al.* (eds.) (2001).

3. Are There Any Signs of Recovery? BBC News, 16 April 2009. Available at http://news.bbc.co.uk/2/hi/business/8000062.stm.

   Christopher Wood (2009). Is the U.S. Economy Turning Japanese? *The Wall Street Journal,* 26 October.

4. Worse than Japan? *The Economist*, 14 February 2009.

5. Kename Akamatsu (1962). A Historical Pattern of Economic Growth in Developing Countries, *Journal of Developing Economies*, 1(1): 3–25.

   Edith Terry (2002). *How Asia Got Rich — Japan, China, and the Asian Miracle,* Armonk, New York: M.E. Sharp Publishing.

   Terutomo Ozawa (2005). *Institutions, Industrial Upgrading, and Economic Performance in Japan — The 'Flying-Geese', Paradigm of Catch-Up Growth,* Northampton, Massachusetts: Edward Elgar Publishing.

6. Rameshwar Tandon (2005). *The Japanese Economy and the Way Forward*, New York: Palgrave Macmillan.

7. Magnus Blomström, Byron Gangnes and Sumner laCroix (eds.) (2001). *Japan's New Economy*, Oxford: Oxford University Press.

8. Hiroshi Yoshikawa (2001). *Japan's Lost Decade*, Tokyo: The International House of Japan.

9. National Academy of Engineering (1987). *Strengthening U.S. Engineering through International Cooperation: Some Recommendations for Action*, Washington, DC: National Academy Press.

10. Hiroshi Shibuya, Makoto Maruyama and Masamitsu Yasaka (ed.) *Japanese Economy and Society Under Pax-Americana,* Tokyo: University of Tokyo Press.

11. Ryuichiro Tachi (1993). *The Contemporary Japanese Economy — An Overview,* Tokyo: University of Tokyo Press.

12. Rameshwar Tandon (2005). *The Japanese Economy and the Way Forward*, New York: Palgrave Macmillan.

13. Ryuichiro Tachi (1993). *The Contemporary Japanese Economy — An Overview,* Tokyo: University of Tokyo Press.

    Peter Drucker (1998). In defense of Japanese Bureaucracy, *Foreign Affairs*, 77, 68–80.

14. Kochi Hamada (1995). Bubbles, Busts and Bailouts. In *The Structure of Japanese Economy.* Mitsuaki Okabe (ed.) London: Macmillan, pp. 263–286.

15. Charles Kindleberger (1978). *Manias, Panics, and Crashes: A History of Financial Crisis*, New York: Basic Books.

16. W McKibbin (1996). The Macroeconomic Experience of Japan since 1990: An Empirical Investigation, Research School of Pacific and Asian Studies, Australian National University, quoted in Magnus Blomström *et al.* (ed.) (2001).

17. Japan's National Debt up to 836 Trillion Yen at End of June, *Japanese News Review,* 24 August 2007. Available at http://www.japannewsreview.com/business/business/20070824page_id=1735.

    The Big Sweat, *The Economist*, 13 June 2009.

    Stuck in Neutral, *The Economist*, 15 August 2009.

18. Bill Emmott (2008). *Rivals*, London: Penguin Books.

19. Peng Er Lam (2009). Declining Fertility Rates in Japan: An Ageing Crisis Ahead, *East Asia*, Vol. 26, pp. 177–190.

20. Worse than Japan? *The Economist*, 14 February 2009.

21. Jennifer Amyx (2000). Political Impediments to Far-reaching Banking Reforms in Japan: Implications for Asia.

In *The Asian Financial Crisis and the Architecture of Global Finance*, Gregory Noble and John Ravenhill (eds.), Cambridge: Cambridge University Press.

22. Dick Beason and Jason James (1999). *The Political Economy of Japanese Financial Markets: Myths Versus Reality*, London: Macmillan.

23. Richard C Koo (2009). *The Holy Grail of Macroeconomics*, revised and updated edition, Singapore: John Wiley.

24. *Ibid.*, p. 9.

25. Jennifer A Amyx (2000).

26. Adam Posen (1998). *Restoring Japan's Economic Growth*, Washington DC: Institute for International Economics.

27. Hiroshi Yoshikawa (2001). *Japan's Lost Decade*, Tokyo: The International House of Japan, pp. 98–99.

28. Ronald McKinnon and Kenichi Ohno (1997). *Dollar and Yen: Resolving Economic Conflict between the United States and Japan*, Cambridge, Mass.: MIT Press, 1997.

29. Paul A Volcker and Toyoo Gyohten (1992). *Changing Fortunes : The world's Money and the Threat to American Leadership*, New York: Times Books.

   Ronald McKinnon and Kenichi Ohno (1997). *Dollar and Yen: Resolving Economic Conflict Between the United States and Japan*, Cambridge, Mass.: MIT Press, 1997.

30. Hiroshi Yoshikawa (2001). *Japan's Lost Decade*, Tokyo: The International House of Japan, p. 101.

31. *Ibid.*

32. Stuck in Neutral, *The Economist*, 15 August 2009.

33. Hiroshi Yoshikawa (2001). *Japan's Lost Decade*, Tokyo: The International House of Japan, p. 5.

34. Paul Krugman (1998). *Japan's trap*. Available at http://web.mit.edu/krugman/www/japtrap.html.

Hiroshi Yoshikawa (2001). *Japan's Lost Decade*, Tokyo: The International House of Japan.

Stuck in Neutral, *The Economist*, 15 August 2009.

35. Hiroshi Yoshikawa (2001). *Japan's Lost Decade*, Tokyo: The International House of Japan, pp. 14–15.

36. *Ibid*, p. 15.

37. Mototada Kikkawa (1998). *Manee Haisen* (Money Defeat), Tokyo: Bunshun Shinsho, quoted in Jennifer Amyx (2000).

Rameshwar Tandon (2005). *The Japanese Economy and the Way Forward*, New York: Palgrave Macmillan.

38. Stuck in Neutral, *The Economist*, 15 August 2009.

39. Richard Koo (2009). p. 127.

40. Magnus Blomström, Byron Gangnes and Sumner La Croix (eds.) (2001). *Japan's New Economy*, Oxford: Oxford University Press.

Hiroshi Yoshikawa (2001). *Japan's Lost Decade*, Tokyo: The International House of Japan.

Stuck in Neutral, *The Economist*, 15 August 2009.

41. quoted in Yoshikawa (2001). pp. 120–121.

42. Hiroshi Yoshikawa (2001). *Japan's Lost Decade*, Tokyo: The International House of Japan.

43. Lam Peng Er, Private Communications.

44. Yishay Yafeh (2003). An International Perspective of Corporate Groups and Their Prospects. In Magnus Blomström *et al.* (ed.) (2001).

45. Magnus Blomström, M *et al.* (eds.) (2001).

46. Hiroshi Yoshikawa (2001). *Japan's Lost Decade*, Tokyo: The International House of Japan, p. 112.

47. Ryuichiro Tachi (1993). *The Contemporary Japanese Economy — An Overview,* Tokyo: University of Tokyo Press.

48. Richard C Koo (2009). *The Holy Grail of Macro-economics*, revised and updated edition, Singapore: John Wiley.

49. Magnus Blomström, Jennifer Corbett, Fumio Hayashi and Ani Kashyap (eds.) (2003). *Structural Impediments to Growth in Japan*, Chicago:Chicago University Press, p. 4.

50. Joseph Schumpeter (1934). *The Theory of Economic Develop- ment*, Boston: Harvard University Press.

51. Lee Branstetter and Yoshiaki Nakamura (2001). Is Japan's Innovative Capacity in Decline? In Magnus Blomström *et al.* (eds.) *Structural Impediments to Growth in Japan*, Chicago:Chicago University Press, p. 183.

52. Nothing to Lose but Their (Restaurant) Chain, *The Economist*, 7 February 2009.

53. Peter Drucker (1998). In Defense of Japanese Bureaucracy, *Foreign Affairs*, 77(5), 68–80.

54. Peter S Goodman (2009). Japanese, Prodded to Accept Failure, Say Enough is Enough, *International Herald Tribune*, 7 September, p. 15.

55. Japanese Cellular Phones FAQ. Available at http://euc.jp/misc/cellphones.en.html#import.

56. Magnus Blomström *et al.* (eds.) (2001). *Structural Impediments to Growth in Japan*, Chicago: Chicago University Press, p. 20.

57. Peter Drucker (1998). In Defense of Japanese Bureaucracy, *Foreign Affairs,* 77(5), 68–80.

58. Lessons from a "Lost Decade," *The Economist*, 23 August 2008.

59. Lessons from a "Lost Decade," *The Economist*, 23 August 2008.

60. Worse than Japan? *The Economist*, 14 February 2009.

61. Robert Guest (2009). Red Tape and Scissors, *The Economist*, 30 May 2009.

62. Peter Drucker (1998). In Defense of Japanese Bureaucracy, *Foreign Affairs,* 77(5), 68–80.

63. Hiroshi Yoshikawa (2001). *Japan's Lost Decade*, Tokyo: The International House of Japan, p. 2.

64. Rameshwar Tandon (2005). *The Japanese Economy and The Way Forward*, New York: Palgrave Macmillan.

65. Magnus Blomström and Sumner La Croix (2006). *Institutional Change in Japan*, London: Routledge.

66. The case for such a cultural and intellectual revival for Asia and China is discussed below:

   Heng Siam-Heng (2007). Asian Renaissance and Enlightenment — Problems and Prospects, *Akademika*, 71, 117–123.

   Heng Siam-Heng (2008). China's Cultural and Intellectual Rejuvenation, *Asia Europe Journal*, 6, pp. 401–412.

67. Magnus Blomström, Byron Gangnes and Sumner La Croix (eds.) (2001). *Japan's New Economy*, Oxford: Oxford University Press.

68. Japan's Break with Past on Climate, BBC News, 7 September 2009. Available at http://news.bbc.co.uk/2/hi/science/nature/8241609.stm.

69. Louis Putterman and Dietrich Rueschemeyer (eds.) (1992). *State and Market in Development: Synergy or Rivalry?* London: Lynne Rienner Publishers, p. 245.

Chapter Five

Special Features of the 2008 Crisis[a]

Blessed are the young, for they shall inherit the national debt.

— Herbert Hoover[1]

We are almost daily reminded by the mass media that the 2008 financial crisis is the worst in our life time, the worst since the Great Depression in the 1930s. To get a better feel of how bad the situation is, it may be useful to look at the following:

- The bailouts in the crisis so far are the biggest in history of bailouts.

- It is the first crisis of globalization.[2] It is a downturn is that unusually synchronized around the world.[3]

- It is "once-in-a-half-century, probably once-in-a-century type of event" — as described by former

---

[a]This chapter is based on a talk with the same title given at the Singapore Chinese Chamber of Commerce on 25 June 2009. A shorter version of the chapter appeared as "Extraordinary Features of the Financial Crisis" in the August–September 2009 issue of *Today's Manager*, a Singapore management magazine.

chairman of American Federal Reserve Alan Greenspan.[4]

- The current financial crisis was not caused by some external shock such as OPEC raising the price of oil or a particular country or financial institution defaulting. To quote the words of George Soros, "The crisis was generated by the financial system itself."[5]

- Based on total real GDP, the year 2009 was projected to experience the first contraction in global economy since 1960, according to the IMF World Economic Outlook released in April 2009.[6]

- For the first time, the Federal Reserve Bank (US Central Bank) has become a direct lender to business firms and consumers.

- Up to $60 trillion of nominal protection was sold against an outstanding stock of corporate bonds of just $6 trillion. Between them, these amounted to the biggest asset and credit bubble in human history.[7]

- It is the first international financial crisis in which the IMF has stayed away from trying to tackle the causes of the problem and has played only a secondary part in managing its consequences.

- The Dow Jones Industrial Average dropped by more than 50 percent from 14,165 (highest) on the close of 9 October 2007 to 6,547 on the close of 9 March 2009.

- Unemployment in the USA is almost 9 percent in May 2009 and the OECD predicts that it will reach 10.3 percent in 2010.[8]

- Britain has experienced the first bank-run since the 1870s when the country experienced an ultra-long economic depression lasting 23 years (1873–1896).[9]

- The Royal Bank of Scotland has suffered the biggest loss in British corporate history.[10]

- The collapse of 158-year-old Lehman Brothers on 15 September 2008 is the largest bankruptcy in US business history.

The Size of the Rescues and Their Likely Consequences

Of the special features listed above, the most striking is the size of the amount of money committed to deal with the crisis. The total costs for banks and other financial institutions on assets that originated in the USA, Europe, and Japan could reach $4.1 trillion in the period 2007–2010, according to the IMF in its *Global Financial Stability Report* released in April 2009. Some of these writedowns have already been taken.[11]

Below are the figures for costs to be shouldered by the USA and Great Britain.[12] In early 2008, such figures would have been thought unimaginable. The sight is almost surreal.

The GDP of USA in 2007 is $13.8 trillions

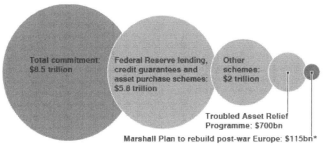

Total commitment: $8.5 trillion

Federal Reserve lending, credit guarantees and asset purchase schemes: $5.8 trillion

Other schemes: $2 trillion

Troubled Asset Relief Programme: $700bn

Marshall Plan to rebuild post-war Europe: $115bn*

*Adjusted for inflation

SOURCE: Bloomberg, US Treasury, Federal Reserve, US National Archive

Some Big Numbers

Jim Bianco of Bianco Research provides some of the big ticket items in American history, the figures have been inflation adjusted.[13]

- *Marshall Plan*: Cost: $12.7 billion, inflation-adjusted cost: $115.3 billion.

- *Louisiana Purchase*: Cost: $15 million, inflation-adjusted cost: $217 billion.

- *Race to the Moon*: Cost: $36.4 billion, inflation-adjusted cost: $237 billion.

- *S&L Crisis*: Cost: $153 billion, inflation-adjusted cost: $256 billion.

- *Korean War*: Cost: $54 billion, inflation-adjusted cost: $454 billion.

- *The New Deal*: Cost: $32 billion (Estimated), inflation-adjusted cost: $500 billion (estimated).

- *Invasion of Iraq*: Cost: $551 billion, inflation-adjusted cost: $597 billion.

- *Vietnam War*: Cost: $111 billion, inflation-adjusted cost: $698 billion.

- *NASA*: Cost: $416.7 billion, inflation-adjusted cost: $851.2 billion.

- *Total*: $3.92 trillion.

The present bailout schemes cost $5.8 trillion, more than the cost of World War II at $3.6 trillion, adjusted for inflation.

UK RESCUE PLANS

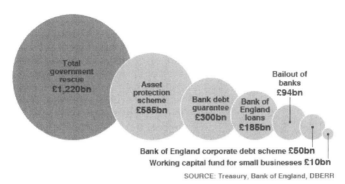

Total government rescue £1,220bn

Asset protection scheme £585bn

Bank debt guarantee £300bn

Bank of England loans £185bn

Bailout of banks £94bn

Bank of England corporate debt scheme £50bn
Working capital fund for small businesses £10bn

SOURCE: Treasury, Bank of England, DBERR

The total GDP of the UK in 2007 is $2.5 trillion (£1.4 trillion).

Bearing in our minds such figures, we are in a better position to understand the gloomy picture painted by Paul Krugman, the 2008 Nobel laureate of economics. In an interview with the BBC on 3 June 2009, he said that the economic slowdown could last 5–10 years and any recovery would be "so slow [that] it would feel like a recession."[14]

There are at least two other pieces of data to support such pessimistic assessment. There are currently about one million excess housing units — a product of the housing boom during the height of the subprime borrowing binge. It takes some time to work away this excess. At the point of writing, the US national debt clock registers $12.35 trillion. Based on an estimated population of 308.6 million, the debt burden per person is $40,000 and $113,000 per taxpayer.[15]

For the USA to get out of crisis, it has to save more, to import less and to export more. It may have to be pragmatic to drop its opposition to exporting to China high-tech such as semi-conductor production plants of the latest generation.

For countries such as Singapore and Malaysia that traditionally rely on the USA as the major export market, they have to recalibrate their export strategies and perhaps even their economic strategies.

The Biggest Asset and Credit Bubble

The pain is not totally over. The credit crunch has been a series of multiple crises, starting with subprime mortgages in America and progressively sweeping through asset classes and geographies. There are now some glimmers of optimism in the investment-banking world, where trading books have already been marked down ferociously and credit exposures to the real economy are more limited. But most banks are hunkering down for more misery, as defaults among consumers and companies spiral. In its latest *Global Financial Stability Report*, the IMF estimates that the total bill for financial institutions will come to $4.1 trillion."[16]

> This crisis is not merely the result of the US housing bubble's bursting or the collapse of the United States' subprime mortgage sector. The credit excesses that created this disaster were global. There were many bubbles, and they extended beyond housing in many countries to commercial real estate mortgages and loans, to credit cards, auto loans, and student loans.

There were bubbles for the securitized products that converted these loans and mortgages into complex, toxic, and destructive financial instruments. And there were still more bubbles for local government borrowing, leveraged buyouts, hedge funds, commercial and industrial loans, corporate bonds, commodities, and credit-default swaps — a dangerous unregulated market wherein up to $60 trillion of nominal protection was sold against an outstanding stock of corporate bonds of just $6 trillion. Taken together, these amounted to the biggest asset and credit bubble in human history....[17]

The costs of this failure are massive. Frantic efforts by governments to save their financial systems and buoy their economies will do long-term damage to public finances. The IMF reckons that average government debt for the richer G20 countries will exceed 100 percent of GDP in 2014, up from 70 percent in 2000 and just 40 percent in 1980.

The US state finance faces fundamental problems. The federal budget, which had a steadily increasing surplus at the end of the 1990s, now has growing deficits. From being a country with a budget in surplus, a strong currency, and a decreasing national debt, the USA has become a country with a long-term budget deficit, a weakening currency, and an increasing national debt. America's national debt has already passed $12 trillion. But this is only the tip of the iceberg of American financial woes, according to Peter Peterson, formerly Commerce Secretary of President Nixon administration. The federal government shoulders burden equivalent to $483,000 per American household, largely in the form of unfunded commitments to provide old people with health care and pensions. Politicians are too concerned with getting elected to face up to the ugly realities, as Peterson has experienced it first hand. He recalls his shock when Bill Clinton, sitting next to him, agreed that social security was bankrupt, and then stood up to tell a crowd of voters that it was just fine.[18]

Away from the Rich Countries

The crisis is testing the resolve of rich countries to hold on to their proclaimed belief in free trade and enlightened political values. There are voices calling for protectionist measures as a way to cope with the crisis. Though their governments show tendency to listen to such voices, so far they have by and large stuck to their commitment to promote free trade and investment.

On the other hand, private capital flow into emerging markets is declining, which suggests that globalization is under strain. From a peak of $929 billion in 2007, net inflow of private capital is projected to slow to $165 billion in 2009, according to Institute of International Finance. Much of the drop is accounted for by the flight of money from the capital markets. There is also a net outflow of bank funds as borrowers pay back more than they borrow.[19]

At the same time, it is disturbing to note that people are becoming more susceptible to xenophobic views. For electoral reasons, mainstream politicians may shy away from confronting extremist politicians. Worse still they may succumb to the opportunistic tactic of echoing far-right rhetoric about immigrants.

In March 2009, the IMF Managing Director Dominique Strauss-Kahn warned that the world was gripped by a great recession that could throw millions back into poverty across the African continent. The economic crisis raised "the threat of civil unrest, perhaps even a war." "The IMF expects global growth to slow below zero this year, the worst performance in most of our lifetimes," he said. He called upon wealthy Western countries to maintain financial support for low-income nations.[20]

In particular, emerging market risks have risen the most in the past six months, the IMF says in its Global Financial Stability Report released in April 2009. The retrenchment of capital flows is straining economies that have relied on foreign-financed credit growth. At the same time, the deteriorating economic environment has increased expected bank write downs and raised the need for fresh capital in emerging market banks, according to José Viñals, Financial Counsellor and Director of the fund's Monetary and Capital Markets Department.[21] In the words of Roger Altman, a former US Deputy Treasury Secretary[22]:

> Countries in Africa have been hardest hit of all, and instability will likely rise there. Fragile states, such as the Democratic Republic of the Congo and the Central African Republic, have seen their social problems exacerbated by the crisis. Foreign reserves in the region have dwindled. The Congolese government will soon be unable to import essentials, such as food and fuel. The Central African Republic is already unable to pay the salaries of its civil servants... A World Bank study estimated that 53 million people

living in emerging markets will fall back into absolute poverty this year. More frightening, according to the same study, up to 400,000 more children will die each year through 2015 on account of this economic crisis.

First Crisis of Globalization

The peso crisis of Mexico in 1994 affected Mexico and threatened to engulf other Latin American countries. The Asian financial crisis of 1997 was much bigger in magnitude and scope but it did not seriously affect Western Europe and the USA for long. The Japanese bubble lasted over a decade but its impact on the Latin American countries was not deep. These crises are international in character but compared to what the world experiences now, they are much more limited in scope.

In the current crisis, America is spreading the burden of its housing bubble across the whole globe. Foreigners hold a big chunk of American mortgage-based securities. Sovereign wealth funds have injected funds into American banks. The current economic crisis is the first truly serious *global* financial crisis since the advent of globalization. It hits *very seriously and more or less simultaneously* both the advanced industrial economies and the emergent economies.

The international financial system in its present form is a product of deregulation, globalization, and advanced information technology. It is also the most advanced aspect of globalization. It is perceived to be a major factor propelling globalization — in promoting trade and investment. Since the advent of globalization a few decades ago, banking is seen as an industry that embodies the free market ideology associated with glob-alization. As it has turned out, banks in Western countries exist at the largesse of their governments.[23] Moreover, governments have bullied the accounting bodies to change accounting standards to help the banks.

The global financial system is supposed to contribute to the wealth of nations all over the world. Instead it has served as a conveyor belt bringing the ills that originated in Wall Street to every corner of the world. The system was under so much strain that some feared that it could collapse. "October [2008] was the most uncomfortable moment in my career," recalls Gordon Nixon, the head of Royal Bank of Canada. "There was a possibility that the entire system could go under."[24]

In its World Economic Outlook report released in April 2009, the IMF says that this downturn is unusually synchronized around the globe. Recoveries from globally synchronized recessions take 50 percent longer than other recoveries.

The crisis provides a unique occasion for us to look at the European Union and the euro as phenomena of glob-alization. Would it spur economic reform and whether it will attract more members to the club, or whether some of them will think of leaving? The crisis is proving by far the biggest test to date for the euro zone. Both the EU and the euro have withstood the test very well. No EU member has shown any tendency to leave the Union. Similarly, the crisis increased the appeal of the euro. Denmark, Sweden, Bulgaria, and the three Baltic states peg their currencies to the euro. Bulgaria and the three Baltic States, Poland, Hungary, Czech, and Romania are keen to enter the zone. As emerging economies, they are victims to sudden change in forex sentiments. Exchange rate stability has special appeal to them.

Moreover, the euro is set to play a greater role as an international reserve currency, even though it still has a long way to go to displace the greenback as the main international currency.[25]

Endnotes

1. Herbert Hoover was the 31st President of the United States (1929–1933). The quote is in his address to the Nebraska Republican Conference, Lincoln, Nebraska (16 January 1936). Herbert Hoover [accessed on 30 June 2009]. Available at http://en.wikiquote.org/wiki/Herbert_Hoover.
2. B Emmott (2008). *Rivals,* London: Penguin.
3. The IMF (2009). World Economic Outlook April 2009 [accessed on 30 June 2009]. Available at http://www.imf.org/external/pubs/ft/weo/2009/01/pdf/text.pdf.
4. Edward Carr (2009). Greed — and fear, *The Economist*, 24 January 2009.
5. George Soros (2008). The Crisis & What to Do about It, New York Review of Books, 4 December 2008.
6. The IMF (2009). World Economic Outlook April 2009 [accessed on 30 June 2009]. Available at http://www.imf.org/external/pubs/ft/weo/2009/01/pdf/text.pdf.
7. Nouriel Roubini (2009). Warning: More Doom Ahead, Jan/Feb 2009 *Foreign Policy* [accessed on 30 June 2009]. Available at http://www.foreignpolicy.com/story/cms.php?story_id=4591.
8. Robert Guest (2009). Creative Destruction, *The Economist*, 30 May 2009.

9. Edward Carr (2009). Greed — and fear, *The Economist*, 24 January 2009. Samuel Berrick Saul (1969). The Myth of the Great Depression, London: Macmillan.

10. RBS posted a net loss of £24.1 billion for the year 2008, attributable mainly to its purchase of the Dutch bank ABN AMRO. The bank had a profit of £7.3 billion a year earlier. The loss was smaller than analysts had expected, but it stunned many Britons as a record-setting benchmark of corporate disaster. Prior to RBS's announcement, the biggest annual loss of any UK corporation was the £14.9 billion loss reported by Vodafone in 2006.

    RBS Reports Record Corporate Loss [accessed on 30 June 2009]. Available at http://news.bbc.co.uk/2/hi/business/7911722.stm.

    Julia Werdigier (2009). Record Loss at Royal Bank of Scotland, *The New York Times*, 26 February 2009. [accessed on 30 June 2009]. Available at http://www.nytimes.com/2009/02/27/business/worldbusiness/27rbos.html.

11. Peter Dattels and Laura Kodres (2009). Further Action Needed to Reinforce Signs of Market Recovery: IMF, 21 April 2009 [accessed on 30 June 2009]. Available at http://www.imf.org/external/pubs/ft/survey/so/2009/RES042109C.htm.

12. Global Downturns: in graphics, 19 March 2009 [accessed on 30 June 2009]. Available at http://news.bbc.co.uk/2/hi/business/7893317.stm.

13. Barry Ritholtz, Big Bailouts, Bigger Bucks, 25 November 2008. [accessed on 25 January 2009]. Available at http://www.ritholtz.com/blog/2008/11/big-bailouts-bigger-bucks/.

14. Krugman Fears Prolonged Slowdown, 3 June 2009 [accessed on 30 June 2009]. Available at http://news.bbc.co.uk/2/hi/business/8081813.stm.

15. US National Debt Clock, [accessed on 31 January 2010] Available at http://www.usdebtclock.org/.

16. Andrew Palmer (2009). Rebuilding the Banks, *The Economist*, 16 May 2009.

17. Nouriel Roubini (2009). Warning: More Doom Ahead, January/February 2009 *Foreign Policy* [accessed on 20 June 2009]. Available at http://www.foreignpolicy.com/story/cms.php?story_id=4591.

18. America's Fiscal Cassandra, *The Economist*, 6 June 2009.

19. Homeward Bound, *The Economist*, 7 February 2009.

20. 'Great Recession' Could Spark Civil Unrest, IMF Chief Tells France 24 [accessed on 20 June 2009]. Available at http://www.france24.com/en/20090310-imf-strauss-kahn-great-recession-world-economy-financial-crisis.

21. Peter Dattels and Laura Kodres (2009). Further Action Needed to Reinforce Signs of Market Recovery: IMF, 21 April 2009 [accessed on 20 June 2009]. Available at http://www.imf.org/external/pubs/ft/survey/so/2009/RES042109C.htm.

22. Roger C Altman (2009). Globalization in Retreat. *Foreign Affairs*, 88(4), pp. 2–7.

23. Andrew Palmer (2009). Exit Right, *The Economist*, 16 May 2009.

24. Andrew Palmer (2009). Rebuilding the Banks, *The Economist*, 16 May 2009.

25. John O'Sullivan (2009). Holding Together, *The Economist*, 13 June 2009.

Chapter Six

Bonfire of Financial Excesses

The market can stay irrational longer than you can stay solvent.

— John Maynard Keynes[1]

Introduction

Financial crises are generally preceded by financial excesses. The excesses take a plethora of forms such as high leverages, fancy derivatives, and dysfunctional salaries and bonuses. Performance pressure, wrong incentives, and use of fancy financial instruments in a lightly regulated setting have combined to pervert the proper roles of financial markets. Moreover, they have seriously weakened the financial systems of countries badly hit by the crisis. It is argued that of all the factors that are directly implicated in the excesses, the main one is deregulation. Though there was regulation in the formal sense, what happened in practice was light regulation and lax supervision or even no regulation in the case of shadow banking. The primary purpose of regulation is to protect the public and business firms, and not to promote the interests of the financial sector.

Perhaps the following passages taken from the pro-market newspaper *The Economist* may serve as a gentle introduction to the financial excesses of Wall Street and the City of London.[2]

> The monument to Soviet central planning was supposed to have been a heap of surplus left boots without any right ones to match them. The great bull market of the past quarter century is commemorated by millions of empty houses without anyone to buy them. Gosplan drafted workers into grim factories even if their talents would have been better suited elsewhere. Finance beguiled the bright and ambitious and put them to work in the trading rooms of Wall Street and the City of London. Much of their effort was wasted. You can only guess at what else they might have achieved.
>
> When the financial system fails, everyone suffers. Over the past 22 months the shock has spread from American housing, sector by sector, economy by economy. Some markets have seized up; others are being pounded by volatility. Everywhere good businesses are going bankrupt and jobs are being destroyed. For the first time since 1991 global average income per head is falling.... Financial markets promised prosperity; instead they have brought hardship. Financial services are in ruins. Perhaps half of all hedge funds will go out of business. Without government aid, so would many banks....

It is interesting to read how the failures of rigidly planned economy of the Soviet Union are compared with the results of the financial excesses of Anglo-American free market economy. At the same time, it is a mild cultural shock to read the languages used by the mass media to describe the banking industry before and after the crash. At the height of the boom, bankers and financial wizards were profiled as creators of immense wealth and do-gooders. They flew around in corporate jets because their time was so precious. Their contributions were so enormous that they were rewarded astronomical salaries and bonuses. They were hailed as masters of the universe. Former Fed chairman Alan Greenspan was praised for his pragmatism, flexibility, and shrewd judgment. At one point, he was nearly branded the God of Money. He was celebrated as the "Maestro" in a book about him by Bob Woodward. After the crash, they are seen as irresponsible, incompetent, greedy, and destroyers of wealth. Sir Fred Goodwin (former head of Royal Bank of Scotland) and other bankers like him represent everything that went wrong with the system. They have become disgraced, a focal point of public anger and disdain.

Some Attributes of Financial Excesses

A financial crisis is preceded by some form of financial excesses. In the midst of the Dutch tulip mania, a tulip was valued at more than a house.[3] In recent years, the world has seen at least three major bubbles — the bubble economy of Japan, the dot-com bubble, and the US sub-prime mortgage bubble. In early 1990, the market capitalization of Japan exceeded that of the USA, even though the later had twice Japan's population and GDP.[4] The dot-com euphoria focused on market share even though dot-com companies were burning shareholders' money and bank loans to enlarge their market shares. The exuberance even produced the clever argument that the advanced economies were crossing the boundary of industrial economy into post-industrial economy with a new mode of production and consumption; it was a new economy with its knowledge-based society. In fact, previous bubbles suggest that financial excesses and radical departures from economic and business fundamentals are manifestations of an imminent financial crisis.

The 2008 bubble has its subprime housing mortgages, credit card debts, car loans, student loans, current account deficits, fiscal deficits, and two hemorrhaging wars in Iraq and Afghanistan. Now, some figures to give an indication of the size of the bubble. The debts of American firms rose steadily from 39 percent of GDP in 1988 to 111 percent of GDP in 2008.[5] Outside the traditional banking system, a parallel banking system or shadow banking system has been operating. The financial institutions of the shadow banking system were not regulated at all, and they grew big enough to rival or even to surpass conventional banking in importance.[6] They were the important players brewing alphabet soup of fancy financial products in a runaway financial system. The share of household and consumer debt alone went up from 100 percent of GDP in 1980 to 173 percent in early 2009, equivalent to around $6 trillion of extra borrowing.[7]

In 2007, some $45 trillion of derivative contracts were traded on the S&P 500 indexes alone. That was four and a half times the total value of American stock market of $10 trillion. According to the Bank for International Settlements, the notional value of all outstanding global derivative contracts at the end of 2007 stood at $600 trillion, some eleven times the world economic output.[8] A decade earlier it had been only $75 trillion, and 2.5 times global GDP. The fastest growing part of these markets was credit-default swaps. The notional value of credit default swaps almost doubled in 2007 to $62 trillion.[9]

The money market is supposed to be the best institution to channel idle capital to productive investment. In reality, it has its dysfunctional element that behaves very much like a casino. Just consider the case of naked credit default swaps or CDSs whose buyers do not own the underlying bonds. According to *The Economist*, up to 80 percent of CDSs are naked.[10] It is like four strangers buying insurance coverage of your house even though they do not own it. In theory at least, they can conspire to bring down a company and thereby profit from its bond default. Given the size of the market, those who have an honest interest in protecting their bond purchase would worry whether the CDS sellers are able to honor the contract when called upon to do so.

The frenzy and massive speculation in the context of structural problems in the US economy suggests that the financial crisis of 2008 is an accident waiting to happen. Unlike the Asian financial crisis, which took people by surprise, the current crisis was anticipated by at least several well-respected voices even though they might differ as to the scale and time. As early as 2002, Sheila Bair, currently head of Federal Deposit Insurance Corporation, was among the first to sound the alarm bells about sloppy mortgage-lending and lax regulation.[11]

It is therefore surprising for Robert Rubin to say that no one anticipated the financial crisis. Mr. Rubin is no ordinary banker. He ran the investment firm Goldman Sachs before he became the Treasury Secretary of the Clinton administration, after which he joined Citigroup as a high-level adviser and director.[12] The reality is that in those triumphant days of rising stock market and house prices, the "light touch" regulation of the financial system continued to enjoy approval across broad political spectrum. People preferred to listen to the reassuring words of Alan Greenspan and his likes. This grandee of masters of the universe declared that any major decline in house prices would be most unlikely. There might be some froth in local markets, but there was no national housing bubble.[13] "Because of the housing boom and the accompanying explosion in new mortgage products," he says, "the typical American household ended up with a more valuable home and better access to the wealth it represented. Its mortgage is bigger too, of course, but since debt carries a lower interest rate, the drain on income from debt service as a share of homeowner income did not change much between 2002 and 2005."[14]

The Pressure to Perform

Greed is one word that appears very frequently in the literature on financial crises. It is used to describe the behavior of reckless investors, investment managers, and bankers who gamble with their clients' and shareholders' money. But how can this happen in financial firms if we are to believe management textbooks? There are checks and controls to make sure that financial firms do not take undue risks. Obviously, reality is much more complicated than the neat picture conveyed by textbooks. To begin with, it is quite natural for private investors, investment funds, and pension funds to seek good returns for their investments. It is also understandable that investment managers and investment banks would have to perform well in competitive environment.

It is a well-known fact that it is easy to make money in a bull market. The corollary is that it is difficult to make money during a market downturn. (Of course, one can still do so by selling short.) In addition, it is during a bull market that things tend to get wrong. A time-honoured strategy to make more money is through volume or growth. The idea is transmitted by senior managers to their staff to demand double-digit increases in sales and profits year in, year out. The growth imperative required volumes for each product to be big, as they were in mortgage-backed securities and leveraged loans. Some of the worst mistakes befell banks such as Citigroup, UBS, and Merrill Lynch that were instructed by the top to catch up in mortgage finance.[15] But an indiscriminate use of such strategy can lead to disaster. This is what has happened to UBS, as revealed by its internal investigation into $38 billion of mortgage losses. Under pressure to grow in the fixed income business, the collateralized debt obligations (CDO) desk went for "mezzanine" tranches of the securities.[16] The fancy financial products paid more but ultimately lost more too. At its peak, the CDO desk had only 35–40 people, but it was responsible for around $12 billion of write-downs in 2007, two-thirds of that year's total.

Besides being speculators themselves, fund managers and investors want others to follow their footpath.

They threaten companies with takeover. They pressure prudent CEOs to do deals in boom periods, to take risks, and to opt for high leverage by taking loans and avoid sitting on mountain of cash. Only companies controlled by families or run by clear-minded executives are able to resist such pressure. One reason is that family-controlled companies are almost impossible to take over because their main shareholders have controlling shares of the companies. Their main shareholders and the managers demonstrate the ability to take decisions guided by long-term view.[18]

What we are witnessing in the run up to the crisis is familiar to those who have been studying business history. For example, read what Peter Drucker describes the hype on the business scene in the 1960s.[19]

> The "financial strategy" that was most popular in the sixties in the U.S. and England, that is, "acquisition by price/earnings ratio" is even unsound as a purely financial maneuver. It is, in fact, not much more than a confidence game. To buy a business not because it makes sense as a business but because the accident of stock-market valuation makes it possible to acquire it and obtain an immediate increase in the buyer's per share earnings — i.e. by paying for a stock with a low price/earnings ratio with a share with a high price/earnings ratio — is financial sleight-of-hand. It creates "leverage," that is, raises apparent earnings per share and with it stock prices in a rising economy and a rising market. Such leverage always works in both directions. In a sagging economy and a sagging stock market such acquisition policy therefore creates at the

slightest setback sharply lower per share earnings and collapsing stock prices. Such an "acquisition policy" is simply another variation of the old game of "pyramiding" that was so popular in the U.S. in the twenties and — deservedly — was outlawed in the thirties, in which companies sold bonds to buy up the shares of other companies.

Bull market also tends to distort a firm's focus and corrupt its governance. The long-term future and real competitive strengths of companies are over-shadowed by concerns to pander to the whims and fancies of the capital market. Everything from sales incentives to budgeting is based on measures aimed at securing a favorable reception of the capital market. It is secondary whether these measures may or may not reveal an honest view of competitive position of the firm. Sometimes, the rot reaches the top, with investors, directors, and managers evaluating performance using cash-flow models designed to dress up quarterly figures. Profits, profits, and again profits. The P-word is what matters. It forms the core of corporate body and soul. In such atmosphere, banks succumb easily to a culture of giving cheap capital to high-risk units.[20]

When the market upturn lasts for a while, people forget the tormenting time of previous bear market. Within the financial and investment community, another set of collective wisdom takes over. For example, KBC Bank of Belgium has the strange practice of combining the roles of chief financial officer and chief risk officer. It is a policy that goes against the most basic of corporate governance standards.[21] The change of wind blows in seeds of accounting shenanigans. The seeds soon sprout. The new seedlings grow and flourish, take deeper and deeper roots, and become a familiar sight.

When it is easy to make money in a bull market, caution is thrown out of the window. A polite reply to those who warn about tail risks[a] is, "Well, you may be right. Just like a clock that has stopped, you are surely right twice a day." Risk managers who persist in maintaining high standards of work are either marginalized or moved upstairs. After a while, only the most determined would wish to voice their concerns that are shrugged off anyway. The climate promotes self-censorship. "The system", says a senior American banker, "filters out the thoughtful and replaces them with the faithful."[22] In such intellectually incestuous climate, bosses, senior managers, and risk managers turn their heads the other way when undue risks are taken by their traders. And these senior people seem to have valid reasons for doing so. After all, the traders are making good money. Do not interfere with their work or they may leave the bank to join the competitor. The situation is certainly made no better by dysfunctional remuneration scheme, which is the subject of the next section.

Excessive credit growth relative to GDP and rapid rises in asset prices have been associated with a weakening of the quality of bank portfolios and an increase in risk exposure. When things take a turn for the worse, the wrong-footed banks begin to lose their bets and capital. They face a different incentive structure from sound

---

[a] Tail risks refer to the rare but devastating events that can bring a bank down. One example of such risks is that encountered by the hedge fund Long-Term Captical Management in 1998.

banks. As they try to recoup their losses, moral hazard increases, particularly when managers do not have their own funds at stake. An unsound bank may offer higher interest rates than its competitors to draw in deposits to pay operating expenses. It may resort to outright gambling by choosing high-risk transactions. In many cases, unsound banks become captive to insolvent debtors or borrowers who have no intention of repaying their debts. Unable to declare loans in default lest they acknowledge their own insolvency, such banks may continue to lend to non-performing borrowers or to capitalize interest on those borrowers' loans.[23]

Remuneration — Professional or Mercenary?

When the cost of borrowing is low and the asset prices are rising generally, it is tempting to use more leverage to earn higher than average profits. The greater the leverage, the greater the profits, and also the greater the risks. Before the recent crash, it was the norm to reward traders based on the profits they generated. Risks were either downplayed and then ignored or supposedly taken care of by sophisticated financial engineering instruments. It is thus easy to see that the incentive system encourages the traders to gamble with the business and to load their firms with toxic securities. "There is now little doubt that pay was a contributory factor in the banking industry's meltdown. Accustomed to fat annual bonuses that were multiples of their base salaries, many bankers had little reason to dwell on the risks associated with the deals that they were signing. Even some of the industry's leading lights, such as Lloyd Blankfein, the head of Goldman

Sachs, have publicly acknowledged that such incentives helped hurl the industry into an abyss.[24] The result was losses that outweighed the profits built up in the good years. For example, Merrill Lynch lost $15.3 billion in the fourth quarter of 2008 alone, compared with the $12.6 billion of post-tax profits it earned in 2005 and 2006 combined.[25]

Such system and practice attract the greedy and the risk-takers — the kind of people who ultimately help to destroy the firms. A friend who has spent his whole working life with an international bank wrote me his observation:

> Take Bear Sterns for instance. They mostly recruited eager, hungry-for-riches lower middle class males willing to do anything to make it big. Whereas an old established investment bank like Lazard Freres took in the more genteel persons, the well connected sons of ambassadors and senior politicians who are accustomed to money and power and not so eager to strike it rich. So they refrained from taking on excessive risks. Bear Sterns concentrated heavily and almost solely on the most lucrative mortgage loans and did not diversify. So they were undone by their own greed. Lazar prudently spread its risks among several lines of business. They made less money, but they also incurred less risk and survive to this very day.

To get an idea of the size of the pay packages dished out to the best and brightest of Wall Street and the City of London at a time when their firms suffered huge losses, let us look at some of the figures reported by the

British Guardian newspaper.[26] From 2000 to 2007, the last chairman and CEO of Lehman Brothers, Richard Fuld, was paid $485million. Merrill Lynch's chairman Stan O'Neal retired after announcing losses of $8 billion, taking a final pay deal worth $161 million in 2007. His CEO colleague John Thain was rewarded with $83 million the same year.[27] Citigroup boss Chuck Prince left in 2007 with a $38 million handshake after the bank incurred multibillion-dollar losses. Bob Diamond, president of the British bank Barclays, received a salary of £250,000, but his total pay reached £36 million in 2007. Just in case the readers need further hint at why some people should be so upset, read some other details in the same Guardian report. The pay package of Morgan Stanley for 2008 was $10.7 billion; it was at one point in October the same year greater than the entire stock market value of the business. At that price, staff could just use their pay to buy the bank!

Another form of such excesses is the kind of perks they expect to enjoy. For example, as CEO of Merrill Lynch, John Thain spent more than $1.2 million of the bank's money renovating his office and two surrounding conference rooms at the firm's lower Manhattan headquarters.[28] In the surreal world of Wall Street, refurbishing one's office with everything from a fireplace to Renaissance painting was a sport in itself.[29] It was certainly not seen as improper by insiders, but rather as a sign of status and good taste.

In its last three years, Bear Stearns paid $11.3 billion in employee compensation and benefits. According to its 2007 annual report, Lehman Brothers shelled out $21.6 billion in the three years before. In 2007, it paid out at least $5.1 billion in cash compensation, equivalent to a third of the core capital left just before it failed. Merrill Lynch paid staff over $45 billion during the three years to 2007. And even when it was suffering $15 billion in losses for the fourth quarter in 2008, it paid out a couple of billion bucks in bonuses to its employees.[30]

Employees in financial firms, who were paid about the same as those in other industries until the early 1980s, pocketed 1.8 times as much in 2007. Have their contributions to the economy increased in the same proportion during the period? Most likely not. It has been estimated that 30–50% of the wage gap between financial and non-financial workers between the mid-1990s and 2006 was the fruit of rent-seeking rather than genuine wealth-creation.[31]

The pay scheme of Wall Street captains is a concentrated expression of what has gone wrong with financial capitalism operating in a free market environment. To the innocent victims of the crisis and unlucky clients of Madoff, there is not even a shadow of professionalism that can underpin Wall Street's claim to trust and respect. Money in vulgar abundance does not seem capable of ensuring competence and integrity. The culture of professionalism has given way to the culture of mercenaries or, worse still, to the culture of crooks.

From Hero to Zero

What has happened at Wall Street provides rich materials of corporate skullduggery for Hollywood movie producers. One is reminded by the 1987 movie *Wall Street* that is about the unscrupulous, cynical, and quick-buck culture of the 1980s. The story is about how unrestrained greed took possession of Wall Street players. In the film, the main character Gordon Gekko uttered the famous line "Greed is good". "Greed is good" credo typifies the short-term view prevalent in the 1980s and Gekko is its embodiment.[32] The problems that existed in the 1980s market have since grown into a much larger phenomenon. The result is the super bubble. And the world is still suffering from the destructive creativities of numerous Gordon Gekkos and their mutations.

Movie script writers can draw on the *modus operandi* of some well-connected bankers — how they rise to become masters of the universe and their subsequent fall from hero to zero. There is certainly no shortage of real life characters to act as sources of inspiration. One such colorful person is Richard S Fuld, Jr. who was the last chairman and CEO of Lehman Brothers. He has by now become a world renowned figure because on his watch the Wall Street icon Lehman Brothers went bankrupt. In November 2008, as he prepared to face lawsuits from angry investors, he sold his Florida mansion standing on three-acre Florida estate to his wife Kathleen for $100. This may protect the house from potential legal actions against him. They had bought it only four years earlier for $13.56 million.[33]

Another inspirational character is John Thain, former CEO of Merrill Lynch. After the troubled investment bank was absorbed by Bank of America, he was dismissed. "Right now, John is radioactive", says Mr. John Reed, the former chairman and CEO of Citicorp Inc. "I would guess any company with a public board would have a hard time hiring him. Bank of America made him the poster boy for bad practices."[34]

Of course, the honor of Father of Perfidy must be reserved for Bernard Madoff. His name may even join that of Ponzi to become part of lexicon of innovative finance.

> In a larger sense, the case of Bernard L. Madoff put an entire era on trial — a heady time of competitive deregulation and globalized finance that climaxed last autumn in a frenzy of fear, panic and loss. The blame for the largest, longest and most widespread Ponzi scheme in history has been spread widely — to arcane credit default swaps, to lax enforcement of weak regulations, to poorly understood risks and to badly managed financial institutions.[35]

Before the Ponzi scheme came to light, he was seen as a senior statesman at Wall Street. He was respected for his vision and trusted by tens of thousands of customers. After his scheme was uncovered and having gone through the due process of court trial, he was sentenced to serve 150 years in prison, the maximum for his white-collar crimes. Madoff is a noble of distinguished linage of corporate malfeasance.[36]

Madoff and like-minded corporate players made use of weaknesses in corporate governance to line their own pockets. For example, former CEO Dennis Kozlowski and former finance chief Mark Swartz of Tyco International were convicted in court on multiple counts of grand larceny (stealing in the eyes of the law), conspiracy, falsifying business records, and securities fraud. Even after they were convicted in court, some people would come to their defence. Someone wrote in Forbes to question the conviction on legal technicalities:

> It's fair to say that Kozlowski and Swartz abused many corporate prerogatives and that they invented new ones just so they could abuse them. They acted like pigs, as a lot of CEOs act like pigs. Still, the larceny charges at the heart of the case did not depend on whether the defendants took the money — they did — but whether they were authorized to take it. Questions of authority are, by nature, legal questions, not questions for jurors.[37]

Loose Monetary Policy Is Not the Main Culprit

The single person who has become the main target of blame is Mr. Alan Greenspan. His critics, including many economists, attack him on two major points. First, he encouraged the housing bubble by keeping interest rates too low for too long. Second, he played an instrumental role in reducing financial regulation to the bare minimum and he failed to curb the explosive growth of risky and often fraudulent mortgage loans. While he is certainly guilty of the second point, one may put up a mitigating defence on his behalf on the first point.

His easy money policy was a response to the market crash in 1987 soon after he became Fed chairman. He did the same to deal with the collapse of the Savings and Loans in 1990, the demise of the hedge fund Long-Term Capital Management in the late 1990s, the bursting of the dot-com bubble, and the 9/11 terrorist attacks. All these are well known. What is often not mentioned is his role in holding down the interest rates in order to support the wars in Iraq and Afghanistan unleashed by President Bush. As a patriotic American, and by virtue of his political affiliation as a Republican, Greenspan dutifully designed a monetary policy for the American Commander-in-Chief to wage the expensive wars.

When inflation was low, the Fed would follow tradition by keeping interest rates low. Though there were calls to raise interest rates to rein in assets bubbles, there was no consensus to use monetary measure for this purpose. Even Professor Nouriel Roubini, certainly no big fan of Mr Alan Greenspan, considered keeping interest too low for too long only a modest misdemeanor. He did not think that high Fed rates would have stopped this frenzy speculation. "Higher interest rates sooner would have made only little difference, especially in a world where long rates and mortgage rates depended more on global factors — that kept such rates low — rather than on monetary policy."[38]

Greenspan did move interest rates up when there was a clear sign of inflation. Before the current crisis, he was credited for steering the American economy through one of the longest booms in history, while also presiding over a period of declining inflation. (Whether he was the lucky enough to be the Fed chairman at the right time is another issue.) Only by bearing this in mind can we understand why he was given loud accolade until recently.

The Central Issue of Regulation

Though Greenspan could defend his monetary policy, he would find it difficult to argue that he did a good job as bank regulator. As a bank regulator, he did not believe in regulation and he did his best to reduce regulations to a minimum. He was well known as a great cheerleader of exotic financial innovations. He did not bother to control credit. And easy credit led to high leverage. Easy credit, high leverage, light regulation, and lax supervision combine to produce ideal conditions for bubble to build up. As George Soros points out:

> Bubbles always involve the expansion and contraction of credit and they tend to have catastrophic conse-quences. Since financial markets are prone to produce bubbles and bubbles cause trouble, financial markets have become regulated by the financial authorities. In the United States they include the Federal Reserve, the Treasury, the Securities and Exchange Commission, and many other agencies.[39]

Among the factors accounting for the financial excesses, the main one is deregulation.[40] Greed, indecent remunerations, easy money and savings glut, and even failures of rating agencies are relatively minor factors. In his recent book, Henry Kaufman, a former Salomon Brothers banker, looks at the past quarter of a century's financial deregulation. He finds that loose regulations led to a loosening of credit standards and questionable inno-vations, particularly the securitization of bank loans, which created the illusion that credit risk could be reduced if the instruments became marketable. Along the way, the public perception of liquidity changed, from one based on assets to one centred on liabilities.[41] In other words, money supply in the market place is not only determined by interest rates but also determined by credit, let loose by deregulation.

Easy credit allows speculation to embark on high-leverage gamble. Good luck means huge profits. The reverse is true too, except that the losses are to be borne by the lender. Remember the apt observation of John Keynes: "If you owe your bank a hundred pounds, you have a problem. But if you owe a million, it has."[42] A similar point is made by the great American economist Irving Fisher. A scholar of the Depression, he warns that over investment and over speculation would have far less serious results were they not conducted with borrowed money. He says, "I fancy that over-confidence seldom does any great harm except when, as, and if, it beguiles its victims into debt."[43]

In fact, over-leverage can result in balance sheet recession, as it has happened with Japanese firms and now with American households and many firms. In terms of growth, the overall economic consequences are worse than the physical wreckage wrought by wars. As soon as a war ends, physical reconstruction can begin immediately, stimulating development and fueling growth. A recession brought about by over leverage decimates the assets but leaves the debts standing. It means that households and firms will have to work themselves out of deep holes. Profits and otherwise disposable incomes are directed to filling the holes. Investment and consumption beyond basic necessities will just have to wait.

As far back as 1994, Greenspan staunchly and successfully opposed tougher regulations on derivatives. In 1999, at a time when he enjoyed immense prestige and influence, he lent his full weight to support the Clinton administration and Congress not to regulate derivatives. In such free-for-all world, the growth of derivatives exploded. Credit default swaps were worth $1 trillion in 2002 and they were worth $33 trillion in 2008. One sad result of such clever financial innovations was the saga of AIG. Without US rescue intervention, the 374 people of its derivative products group in London would have destroyed a company that had 116,000 employees in 120 countries.

On Greenspan's watch, the leverage of banks went from 10-to-1 to 30-to-1. In such background of malign neglect, a shadow banking system took shape. This shadow system consists of financial institutions that are not regulated at all. Typical among them are hedge funds and investment banks.

To get an idea of how high the level of leverage a firm can reach in a deregulated environment, let us look briefly at the famous Long-Term Capital Management, whose speculation nearly caused a meltdown of the global financial systems. According to one account, the hedge fund had at one point in time a capital of $600 million against debts of more than $1 trillion.[44] Another account — this one by Alan Greenspan — has it that LTCM had a $125 billion portfolio and leveraged its bets with more than $125 billion bank loans. "It also carried some $1.25 trillion in financial derivatives, exotic contracts that were partially reflected on its balance sheet." He went on to say that even after the implosion of LTCM and the smoke was cleared, no one ever knew for sure how highly leveraged the hedge fund was when things started to go wrong.[45]

Nobel economics laureate Robert Solow argues that effective limits on leverage, even if they have to be different for different classes of institutions, are basic to controlling the potential instability of the financial system. "Even with more transparency, extreme leverage is what generates extreme uncertainty and systemic risk. And it also encourages the dangerous compensation practices.... Leverage allows a clever player to manage enormous sums; it is then irresistible to focus on the short run and skim off mind-boggling paychecks and bonuses before the opportunity goes away."[46] Asian countries are relatively unscathed this time as compared to what happened to them about a decade ago. Besides huge foreign reserves buildup, it is because their banks are not so highly leveraged. There is control of credit even though their standard of transparency is lower than that of Wall Street.

Using high leverage, the best and brightest graduates from Harvard and MIT designed exotic investment products and highly complex instruments. They tried to speculate for high profits while working away the risks — the financial equivalent of squaring the circle.

The Fed has broad authority to prohibit deceptive lending practices under a 1994 law known as the Home Owner Equity Protection Act. But it took little action during the long housing boom. As a result, less than one percent of all mortgages were subjected to restrictions under the law. Greenspan, together with most other banking regulators in Washington, resisted calls for tighter regulation of subprime mortgages and other high-risk exotic mortgages that allow people to borrow beyond their means.[47]

The regulators believe that the self-interest of non-regulated financial firms would function to protect shareholder's equity. In his testimony to Committee of Government Oversight and Reform on 23 October 2008, Alan Greenspan says, "Such counterparty surveillance is a central pillar of our financial markets' state of balance. If it fails, as occurred this year, market stability is undermined." It is amazing that such an intelligent man seems not to have noticed the behavior of gamblers. Gamblers are surely conscious of their own interests. And they surely do not wish to lose their fortunes when they walk into casinos. Yet they often gamble to bankruptcy and put their families into a state of misery. Self-interest of gamblers has failed to protect them from their own greed and follies. It is with good reason that governments either ban gambling or exercise very tight regulations over casinos.

Neoliberals believe ardently in market rationality. It is fair to assume that rationality includes the ability to learn from one's own or others' mistakes. However, financial market has not exhibited such learning behavior, at least not too well. One may marvel at how quickly Wall Street forgets, as it did after the LTCM episode. Soon it was not only emulating its risky bets but it also expanded their scope.[48]

The demise of LTCM reveals the danger posed by the shadow banking system, but somehow the danger was ignored once the problem was over. There was no attempt to fix the flaw in the deep structure. Instead, the episode was interpreted by Greenspan and other free marketeers that the financial system was very robust.

It is also not that the US administration, lawmakers, and those in charge of financial regulation and supervision have not been informed about the need for regulation. A strong case for it has been succinctly stated by Martin Feldstein, a former president and CEO of the National Bureau of Economic Research and a former chairman of the President's Council of Economic Advisors.

> The banking system as a whole is a 'public good' that benefits the nation over and above the profits that it earns for the banks' shareholders. Systemic risks to the banking system are risks for the nation as a whole. Although the managements and shareholders of financial institutions are, of course, eager to protect the solvency of their own institutions, they do not adequately take into account the adverse effects to the nation of systemic failure. Banks left to themselves will accept more risk than is optimal from a systemic point of view. That is the basic case for government regulation of banking activity and the establishment of capital requirements.[49]

The descent into the current sorry state of affairs is put in a nutshell by Niall Ferguson, a Harvard professor:

> We had the Great Depression, and then we imposed many actually useful regulations, both on the financial system and on the real economy. Some of them became excessive, and even before Reagan and Thatcher, Jimmy Carter started deregulating some parts of the economy. Eventually policy makers started believing that self-regulation is best; but that means no regulation. We believed in market discipline; but there is no discipline when there is irrational

exuberance. We relied on internal risk management models; but nobody listened to risk managers when the risk takers were making all the profits in the banks; and we relied on rating agencies which had massive conflicts of interest since they were being paid by those that they were supposed to be rating. So the entire model of self-regulation and market discipline now has collapsed.[50]

Financial Excesses Weaken Financial Systems

In normal times, people tend to buy the idea that financial markets behave like robust systems. As sound systems, they are able to correct themselves through negative feed-backs. Left to themselves, they tend to swing back to equilibrium and deviations from equilibrium are random. Serious problems are caused by external events such as sudden hikes in oil prices, *coup d'etat* or war. But in the current recession, no extraneous shock can be identified to be the culprit. As pointed out by George Soros, the crisis was generated by the financial system itself and the system collapsed of its own weight.[51] After the bankruptcy of Lehman Brothers, the financial system really ceased to function. It had to be put on life support system. The current crisis represents a powerful case to argue that financial markets are fragile. Indeed, finance systems have become more fragile over the years. There are 139 financial crises between 1973 and 1997 (of which 44 took place in high-income countries), compared with a total of only 38 between 1945 and 1971. Crises are twice as common as they were before 1914.[52] The IMF, in its *World Economic Outlook* of October 2009, counts the cost of 88 banking crises over the past four decades. On the average, seven years after a bust an economy's level of output was almost 10% below where it would have been without the crisis.[53]

A similar view about the fragility of the financial system is expressed by Robert Solow.[54] He says:

> A modern capitalist economy with a modern financial system can probably adapt to minor shocks — positive or negative — with just a little help from monetary policy and mostly automatic fiscal stabilizers: for example, the lower tax revenues and higher spending on unemployment insurance and social assistance that occur in a weakening economy without any need for deliberate action. It is easy to be lulled into the comfortable belief that the system can take care of itself if only do-gooders will leave it alone. But that same financial system has intrinsic characteristics that can make it self-destructively unstable when it meets a large shock.

He gives four characteristics:

1. There is the phenomenon of asymmetric information. Some market players know things that others don't, and can turn that knowledge into profit.
2. Financial engineering can produce securities so complicated and opaque that almost no one in the market can understand their implications.
3. Market cannot be perfect, so the same object can sell for two or more different prices; some market prices can be manipulated by large, informed

operators; some markets take a long time to match supply and demand.

4. Giant financial institutions can raise large sums of credit, in amounts and ways that can affect the whole system, without anyone feeling responsible for the system-wide effects.

The salient feature of the current recession is that it began with banking crisis, and it spread to the rest of the financial sector and then to the rest of the economy. The crisis has ushered in a deep recession and requires massive government bailout and fiscal stimuli. Even in the lucky scenario of a slow recovery, the government is saddled with huge public debts as a result of fiscal stimulus. It will take years for the public debt to be cleared. The problems facing the US are more difficult to solve than those encountered in the past for the following reasons.[55]

- First, clean-ups of the banks are difficult because the complexities of securitization have left toxic assets that range from car loans, student loans, and housing loans to collateralized debt obligations and credit default swaps. They are much harder to unravel, value and manage.

- Second, there are twin financial crashes: one in the regulated banking sector and one in the unregulated or shallow banking sector. The latter refers to the hedge funds and investment banks that were responsible for the securitization boom and high financial leverage. Most of the credit collapse has come from the shrinking securitization. Such collapse is not captured in standard measures of banking distress such as non-performing loans.

- Third, the bust has involved household debt. After the dot-com bubble, business firms were rather cautious. Households account for almost all the non-financial debts since 2000. Household debts are more difficult to restructure than commercial debts. Households are saving up to 3.6 percent of their disposable incomes, an encouraging change of course from negative saving in 2007. This results in drop of household expenditure that would not encourage corporate America to invest more. Any boost in demand has to come from the state, which means more persistent and sustained budget deficits.

Conclusion

By way of conclusion, a few observations may be made in the context of financial excesses and financial crises.

First, the corporate world cannot produce profit growth that far exceeds the growth of the economy. By pressuring corporations to perform the superhuman, it is just a matter of time that things will go wrong. These contradictions are bound to emerge in one form or another, sooner or later. If it is not a case of subprime debacle or AIG collapse, there will be other problems. Subprime debacle and AIG bailouts are just episodes or manifestations of this economic logic.

Second, even though market may exhibit self-regulatory behaviors at the best of times, there are many cases of market failures. As the intellectual father of free market, Adam Smith knows just too well of positive roles of market forces. Yet he explicitly advocates the regulation of banks. He is well aware that bank failures have damaging effects on the economy more generally.[56]

Regulation is more important than transparency, which is so often advocated for good governance. Although transparency is all to the good, transparency itself has a meager record in crisis prevention. Even very transparent markets such as the New York Stock Exchange experience formation and bursting of bubbles.[57]

Third, the economist Hyman Minsky observes that capitalist economies have as normal states of affairs the following attributes: inherently unstable nature, disequilibrium, and unemployment. He says, "The capitalist market mechanism is flawed in the sense that it does not lead to stable price-full employment equilibrium, and the basis of the flaw resides in the financial system."[58] He gives us some profound insights into behavior of financial systems. Long periods of stability breed instability. Good times give borrowers and lenders a false sense of safety resulting in declining risk premium and increasing risk appetite. This tendency exacerbates the pro-cyclicality of booms and busts. As a result, financial markets are inherently unstable. Given the critical role of finance in modern economy, financial instability is at the heart of economic crisis. The ups and downs of economic cycle and fragility of financial systems are magnified by deregulation, globalization, and integration with the help of advanced information technology.

Fourth, frenzy speculation in the stock market diverts funds from productive investment. When A buys a stock from B, money changes hand. B keeps the money in order to wait for an opportunity to return to the stock market.

The overall money supply is not changed. However, there is a shift from "transactions circulation" to "financial circulation" — to use the words of Keynes.[59]

Fifth, at the heights of financial speculation, the stock market becomes the main topic of social conversations. Substantial proportions of teachers, engineers, dentists, doctors, college students, and many others are distracted from their routine productive activities. Just imagine the agony of a patient when her dentist leaves in the midst of a treatment to take phone call from his broker.

Sixth, the financial excesses encourage a most profound suspicion of innovation in matters concerning money and more generally in the field of finance. Excesses thus play a negative role in promoting useful innovations.

Seventh, over-size finance can exercise a corrupting influence on a nation's political life. As pointed out by Paul Krugman, "as the financial sector got increasingly bloated its political clout also grew". The result is a vicious cycle. "So, in fact, deregulation bred bloated finance, which bred more deregulation, which bred this monster that ate the world economy."[60]

Finally, the best and brightest are attracted by high salaries to design destructive complex derivatives rather than to make substantial contribution to knowledge as scientists and researchers. The potential of creative curiosity has been hijacked by Wall Street. Propensity for productive and useful work could become atrophied by emulating the bankers. This waste has been pointed out years ago by John Maynard Keynes.[61]

Speculators may do no harm as bubbles on a steady stream of enterprise. But the position is serious when enterprise becomes bubble on a whirlpool of speculation. When the capital development of a country becomes a by-product of the activities of a casino, the job is likely to be ill-done. The measure of success attained by Wall Street, regarded as an institution of which the proper social purpose is to direct new investment into the most profitable channels in terms of future yield, cannot be claimed as one of the out-standing triumphs of *laissez-faire* capitalism — which is not surprising, if I am right in thinking that the best brains of Wall Street have been in fact directed towards a different object.

Endnotes

1. quoted in Finkelstein, B (2006). *The Politics of Public Fund Investing: How to Modify Wall Street to Fit Main Street*, New York: Touchstone.
2. Edward Carr (2009). Greed — and Fear, *The Economist*, 24 January 2009.
3. Ho Kwon Ping (2008). Developing an East Asian Business Ethos, in *Destructive Creativity of Wall Street and the East Asian Response*, Michael Heng Siam Heng and Lim Tai Wei (eds.), Singapore: World Scientific.
4. Paul Krugman (2009). *The Return of Depression Economics and the Crisis of 2008*, New York: W W Norton.
5. Rearranging the Towers of Gold, *The Economist*, 12 September 2009.
6. Paul Krugman (2009). *The Return of Depression Economics and the Crisis of 2008*, New York: W W Norton.

7. Edward Carr (2009). Fixing finance, *The Economist*, 24 January 2009.

8. Giving Credit Where It Is Due, *The Economist*, 8 November 2008, p. 14.

9. Taming the Beast, *The Economist* ,19 October, 2008, p. 18.

10. Naked Fear, *The Economist*, 8 August 2009.

11. The Bailiff, *The Economist*, 11 October 2008.

Other warnings came from the followings:

Dean Baker, Center for Economic and Policy Research.
Edward Gramlich, Fed banker and author.[11]
James Hamilton, University of California at San Diego.
Henry Kaufman, a Wall Street veteran.
Paul Krugman, Princeton University.
Raghuram Rajan, University of Chicago.
Nouriel Roubini, New York University.
Peter Schiff, a broker-dealer and author.
Robert Schiller, Yale University.

Sources: Edward Carr (2009). Wild-Animal Spirits, *The Economist*, 24 January 2009.

Yale M Braunstein (2009). Give Us the Information Already. Available at http://people.ischool.berkeley.edu/%7Ebigyale/meltdown_bailout_primer_ver11.pdf.

Paul Krugman (2009). *The Return of Depression Economics and the Crisis of 2008*, New York: W W Norton.

George Soros and Judy Woodruff (2008). The Financial Crisis: An Interview with George Soros, New York Review of Book, 15 May 2008.

12. Jeff Madrick (2009). How We Were Ruined and What We Can Do, *New York Review of Book*, 12 February 2009.

13. Paul Krugman (2009). *The Return of Depression Economics and the Crisis of 2008*, New York: W W Norton.

14. Alan Greenspan (2007). *The Age of Turbulence*, New York: The Penguin Press, p. 232.

15. Edward Carr (2009). How to Play Chicken and Lose, *The Economist*, 24 January 2009.

16. Of all the financial instruments to have failed, CDOs have turned out to be among the most devastating.
    Edward Carr (2009). Greed — and Fear, *The Economist*, 24 January 2009.

17. Edward Carr (2009). How to Play Chicken and Lose, *The Economist*, 24 January 2009.

18. The Ties that Bind, *The Economist*, 24 January 2009.

19. Peter Drucker (1973). *Management: Tasks, Responsibilities, Practices*, New York: Harper Business, pp. 707–708.

20. Crash Course, *The Economist*, 28 February 2009.

21. Troubles Erode Confidence in European Lenders, *International Herald Tribune*, 2 July 2009, p. 14.

22. Edward Carr (2009). How to Play Chicken and Lose, *The Economist*, 24 January 2009.

23. CJ Lindgren, G Garcia, and MI Saal (1996). *Bank Soundness and Macroeconomic Policy*, Washington, D.C.: International Monetary Fund, pp. 57–58.

24. Attacking the Corporate Gravy Train, *The Economist*, 30 May 2009.

25. The Bonus Racket, *The Economist*, 31 January 2009.

26. Simon Bowers (2008). Wall Street Banks in $70bn Staff Payout, 17 October [accessed on 29 December 2008]. Available at http://www.guardian.co.uk/business/2008/oct/17/executivesalaries-banking/print.

27. Frank Bass and Rita Beamish (2008). AP Study Finds $1.6B Went to Bailed-Out Bank Execs, 21 December

[accessed on 29 December 2008]. Available at http://biz.yahoo.com/ap/081221/executive_bailouts.html?.v=2.

28. Thain Fires Back at Bank of America, *The Wall Street Journal*, 27 April 2009.

29. Bill Saporito (2009). The Deeper Truth about Thain's Ouster from BofA, *Time Magazine*, 25th January. Available at http://www.time.com/time/business/article/0,8599,1873835,00.html.

30. Bill Saporito (2009). The Deeper Truth about Thain's Ouster from BofA, *Time Magazine*, 25 January.

    Unnatural Selection, *The Economist*, 12 September 2009.

31. From a study conducted by Thomas Philippon of New York University and Ariell Reshef of the University of Virginia. Cited by Robert Guest (2009). The Coming Recovery, *The Economist*, 30 May 2009.

32. The main characters are Gordon Gekko and Bud Fox. Gekko is based at least in part on Ivan Frederick Boesky, a real-life Wall Street dealer who was fined and given jail sentence for insider trading. In the film, Gekko uttered the famous line "Greed is good", believed to be based on a speech given by Boesky at the School of Business Administration of University of California, Berkeley in 1986. He says, "Greed is all right, by the way. I want you to know that. I think greed is healthy. You can be greedy and still feel good about yourself". Bud Fox, a young stockbroker, is desperate to become rich fast, having being seduced and corrupted by the allure of easy money.

33. Richard S Fuld, Jr Available at http://en.wikipedia.org/wiki/Richard_S._Fuld,_Jr.

    Looting Stars, *The Economist*, 31 January 2009.

34. Thain Fires Back at Bank of America, *The Wall Street Journal*, 27 April 2009.
35. Diana B Henriques (2009). A Sense of Resolution as Madoff Sentenced, *International Herald Tribune*, 1 July 2009, p. 13.
36. Bernard Madoff has a list of distinguished predecessors:

> Bernard J. Ebbers of WorldCom masterminded an $11 billion accounting fraud. He was sentenced in 2005 to 25 years of imprisonment.
>
> Walter A. Forbes of Cendent committed fraud and conspired to mislead investors and regulators. He was sentenced in 2006 to 12.6 years.
>
> Samuel Israel III of Bayon Group cheated investors out of $450 million. He was sentenced in 2008 to 20 years.
>
> L. Dennis Kozlowski of Tyco looted the company and deceived investors. He was sentenced in 2005 to a period of 8.3 to 25 years.
>
> Sanjay Kumar of Computer Associates committed a $2.2 billion accounting fraud that inflated sales figures. He was sentenced in 2006 to 12 years.
>
> Lance K. Poulsen of National Century Financial enterprises committed a $3 billion fraud which led to the collapse of the company. He was convicted in 2008 and given 30 year jail sentence.
>
> John J Rigas of Adelphia Communications looted the company he founded and hid more than $2 billion of its debt. He was sentenced in 2004 to 15 years.
>
> Jeffrey K. Skilling of Enron committed fraud and conspired to mislead investors. He was sentenced in 2006 to 24.3 years.

Sholam Weiss of National Heritage Life Insurance milked the company of $125 million. He was sentenced in 2000 to 845 years of jail.

Sources: Diana B Henriques (2009). Madoff Is Sentenced to 150 Years for Ponzi Scheme, 29 June. Available at http://www.nytimes.com/2009/06/30/business/30madoff.html.

Diana B Henriques (2009). A Sense of Resolution as Madoff Sentenced, *International Herald Tribune*, 1 July 2009, p. 13.

Dennis Kozlowski. Available at http://en.wikipedia.org/wiki/Dennis_Kozlowski.

37. Dan Ackman (2005). Tyco Trial II: Verdict First, Law Second, 17 June. Available at http://www.forbes.com/2005/06/17/kozlowski-tyco-verdict-cx_da_0617tycoverdict.html.

38. Nouriel Roubini (2007) Who Is to Blame for the Mortgage Carnage and Coming Financial Disaster? Unregulated Free Market Fundamentalism Zealotry, 19 March. Available at http://www.rgemonitor.com/blog/roubini/184125.

39. George Soros (2008). The Crisis & What to Do about It, *The New York Review of Books*, 4 December.

40. Bill Bradley, Niall Ferguson, Paul Krugman, Nouriel Roubini, George Soros, Robin Wells, *et al.* (2009). The Crisis and How to Deal with It, *New York Review of Books*, 56(10), 11 June.

Paul Krugman (2009). *The Return of Depression Economics and the Crisis of 2008*, New York: W W Norton.

Robert Solow (2009). How to Understand Disaster, *The New York Review* of Books, 56(8), 14 May.

Soros (2008).

41. Henry Kaufman (2009). *The Road to Financial Reformation: Warnings, Consequences, Reforms*, New York: *Wiley*.

42. Quoted in *The Economist* (13 February 1982).
43. Simon Cox (2009). The Long Climb, *The Economist*, 3 October.
44. Robert Skidelsky (2001). The World on a String, *The New York Review of Books*, 48(4), 8 March.
45. Alan Greenspan (2007). pp. 193–194.
46. Robert M Solow (2009). How to Understand Disaster, *The New York Review of Books*, 56(8), 14 May, p. 6.
47. Edmund L Andrews (2008). Greenspan Concedes Error on Regulation, *The New York Times*, 23 October.
48. Bill Bradley, Niall Ferguson, Paul Krugman, Nouriel Roubini, George Soros, Robin Wells, *et al.* (2009). The Crisis and How to Deal with It, *New York Review of Books*, 56(10), 11 June.
49. Martin Feldstein (1991). The Risk of Economic Crisis: An Introduction, in The Risk of Economic Crisis, Martin Feldstein (ed.), Chicago: University of Chicago Press.
50. Bill Bradley *et al.* (2009). The Crisis and How to Deal with It, *New York Review of Books*, 56(10), 11 June.
51. George Soros (2008). The Crisis & What to Do about It, *The New York Review of Books*, 4 December.
52. Edward Carr (2009). Greed — and Fear, *The Economist*, 24 January 2009.
53. IMF (2009). *World Economic Outlook — Sustaining the recovery*, October (accessed 29 October 2009). Available at http://www.imf.org/external/pubs/ft/weo/2009/02/index.htm.
54. Robert M Solow (2009). How to Understand Disaster, *The New York Review of Books*, 56(8), 14 May.
55. Worse than Japan? *The Economist*, 14 February 2009.
56. Martin Feldstein (1991). The Risk of Economic Crisis: An Introduction, in *The Risk of Economic Crisis*, Martin Feldstein (ed.), Chicago: University of Chicago Press.

57. AS Blinder (1999). Eight Steps to a New Financial Order, *Foreign Affairs*, 78(5), 50–63.

58. Quoted in Gory Dymski and Robert Pollin (1994). *New Perspectives in Monetary Macroeconomics: Explorations in the Tradition of Hyman P. Minsky*, Ann Arbor: University of Michigan Press.

59. John M Keynes (1930). *Treatise on Money*, New York: Harcourt Brace.

60. Bill Bradley, *et al.* (2009). The Crisis and How to Deal with It, *New York Review of Books*, 56(10), 11 June.

61. John M Keynes (1936). *The General Theory of Employment, Interest and Money*, New York: Prometheus Books, p. 159.

Chapter Seven

The Moral Economy

John Rich, a country music singer, has become the voice of popular protest. In his song *Shuttin Detroit Down*,[1] he told his listeners:

My daddy taught me in this country everyone's the same
You work hard for your dollar and you never pass the blame
When it don't go your way
Now I see all these big shots whining on my evening news
About how their losing billions and its up to me and you
To come running to the rescue
Well, pardon me if I don't shed a tear
There selling make believe and we don't buy that here
Because in the real world their shuttin Detroit down
While the boss man takes his bonus paid jets on out of town
DCs bailing out them bankers as the farmers auction ground
Yeah, while there living up on Wall Street in that New York City town
Here in the real world their shuttin Detroit down

Here in the real world their shuttin Detroit down
Well that old mans been working in that plant most all
his life
Now his pension plans been cut in half and he cant
afford to die
And its a crying shame, cus he ain't the one to blame
When I looked down to see his calloused hands
Well let me tell you friend it gets me fightin mad

Introduction

The song by John Rich is an example of how the economic dislocation caused by the crisis prompts the questioning of government policies. The crisis has also raised the issues of greed, moral beliefs, and social justice. This chapter touches on two ways of looking at greed in economic life, especially in financial systems. Another moral issue is that of fairness, which is seen as an important aspect of the financial systems. The claim that financial systems are fair is time and again refuted in financial crises whose victims turn out to be the poor and not the rich speculators who cause it. It is almost an article of faith in market economy that workers should be fairly rewarded for their contribution to productivity. But for the past three decades or so, the pay rise of American workers has lagged behind their productivity increase. Such unfair practice has been shown to be a factor in the current crisis.[2] It also seriously undermines social legitimacy of market economy as practiced in the USA. The concept of fairness and equity has never escaped the concern of some towering economists in history — Adam Smith, John Stuart Mill, Alfred Marshall, and Arthur

Pigou. They represent a humanist tradition that has been subverted by neoliberalism. The current crisis has produced some hopeful signs of positive change, even though they have not been taken up in the mainstream business life.

Greed in Economic Life — Two Perspectives

The word "greed" appears frequently when people poured out their disgust at the causes of the financial crisis and its adverse consequences. It is quite obvious that the bubble has been built up by greedy bankers chasing after quick super-profits. Political leaders were fast to condemn the irresponsible behavior of these bankers as reckless and greedy. Journalists have likewise painted them in similar terms. Reacting to events on Wall Street, in the City of London and in other financial centers, President Barack Obama and Prime Minister Gordon Brown have spoken bluntly of the greed and irresponsibility of bankers, hedge-fund managers, and others who have betrayed the system and come close to wrecking it.[3] Even Pope Benedict XVI stepped into the debate over global economic policy, telling followers in St Peter's Square in the Vatican that greed was at the heart of the crisis. "This crisis was born out of greed," the pontiff said.[4]

At the risk of over-simplification, there are two perspectives on the role of greed in the crisis. One perspective places more emphasis on institutional setup. The other perspective argues that values still matter a lot.

According to the first position, it is not fruitful to harp on the greed of the bankers. Greed is part of the human condition. Without the financial deregulation that permits irresponsible credit, the subprime problem would not have festered to the degree that it did. Rather than embarking on a campaign to condemn the greedy traders, it is more rewarding to examine the institutional setup that promotes greed and rewards reckless speculation. Those who hold this view prefer to talk about the misguided belief in self-regulating financial market, lax regulation of a potentially unstable system, compensation mechanisms that positively encouraged risk-taking, and short-term opportunism.[5] The opinion is well articulated by Michael Sandel, a Harvard professor of philosophy:

> Some say the problem is greed, which led to irresponsible risk taking. If this is right, the challenge is to rein in greed, to shore up values of responsibility and trust, integrity and fair dealing; to appeal, in short, to personal virtues as a remedy to market values run amuck.
>
> We might call this diagnosis 'the greed critique'. But the greed critique is flawed or, at best, partial. Markets have always run on self-interest. From the standpoint of economics, there is no real difference between self-interest and greed. Greed is a vice in personal relations, but the whole point of markets is to turn this vice into an instrument of the public good. This is the moral alchemy that markets are said to perform. We learn this from Adam Smith who said, "It is not from the benevolence of the butcher, the brewer or the baker that we expect our dinner, but from their regard to their own self-interest". "We address ourselves not to their humanity", Smith said, "but to their self-love. Nobody but a beggar chooses to

depend chiefly upon the benevolence of his fellow citizens". This was Adam Smith. So it's tempting to say that all we need to do is rein in greed and restore integrity among bankers and business executives and politicians, but this response is mainly hortatory: comforting for a time, but not really much help in rethinking the role that markets play in our societies.[6]

The second position is articulated by Ho Kwon Ping, an entrepreneur in Singapore. He says:

Most commentaries on the source of the current crisis dwell on regulatory failures or excessive risk-taking, but they all fail to situate the analysis within a human context — that it was people who did all these things, and that people always function within a larger socio-cultural context. And people, as any behavioral psychologist will certify, respond strongly to incentives.

Many critics have correctly focused on the perverse pay structure of Wall Street — a highly skewed risk-reward system gone awry — as the root cause of today's problems.

Perverse and highly inequitable compensation structures are not only morally objectionable, but more importantly, they are the obvious symbols of a society's value system. And quaint though it may sound, values do matter even in a highly sophisticated financial system.

Successive financial crises have proven one consistent point — regulation by itself cannot prevent excessive speculation or collusive behavior. Greed fuels any speculative boom and aggravates a bust, but it can only be reined in, not by regulation alone, but by a moral framework, the value system of the entire society, within which business is practiced.[7]

As argued in the previous chapter, regulation is certainly very important. This point is central in explaining why the crisis hits those countries with lax regulation so very hard. Regulation done in the right way does matter a lot. It is part of the effort to build a sound and robust financial system. Having said this, one has to concede that there is a limit to what regulation can do. For example, the regulators must be not fall prey to corruption, a common political disease in many Asian counties. Moreover, banks and financial firms are past masters in exploiting the blind spots and profiting from the loopholes. A crisis of such enormity occurs bacause of many causes. Even well-designed rules are of not much use when the supervision is not properly conducted, as we see in the Madoff case. It may thus be said that while well-designed regulations are important, the integrity and quality of bankers and the people implementing the rules cannot be considered as a secondary issue.

The Issue of Fairness and All That

In his testimony to House Financial Services Committee on 23 September 2009, US Treasury Secretary Timothy Geithner reiterated fairness as an important attribute of the financial system. Referring to the need to reduce the likelihood and potential damage of the failures of major financial firms, he says, "Accomplishing these goals and reducing the need for government support of financial institutions in the future is a fundamental issue of fairness, and it is essential to making the financial system more stable, efficient, and robust."

Is the financial system fair? One simple way is to look at the problems inherent in the *modus operandi* of financial market. Take the case of externalities, often also seen as under-pricing of systemic risk. When two parties make a deal, they factor in the cost to themselves, but not to others. The financial firm, if managed properly, calculates only the potential cost to itself if a loan turns bad, but not the potential adverse impact on the financial system. The cost of this impact to the financial system and even to the global economy can be huge, as illustrated in the debacle of the Long-Term Capital Management. This inherent flaw of current capital markets is well known but not accepted by Wall Street and is ignored by the American and British lawmakers.[8]

Another way is to look at the consequences of many a financial crisis. Without exception, the worst affected in financial crises are those at the very bottom of the economic order. Through no fault of theirs at all, many of them lose their jobs. For those in the poor countries, they face additional problem of price increases of daily necessities because their currencies depreciate. At the same time, their governments would cut back medical and educational expenditures. To these countless innocent victims, the system is certainly not fair. This is a point readily admitted by none other than Alan Blinder. Reflecting on the Asian financial crisis in an article published in *Foreign Affairs*, he says that "financial crises afflict literally hundreds of millions of innocent bystanders who play no part in the speculative excesses but nonetheless suffer when the bubbles burst. The present global financial system manifestly fails to protect these poor people from extreme hazards."[9]

In the same article, Blinder has this to say about the IMF. "The fund pays inadequate attention to the protection of innocents — compared, say, to the protection of creditors who may have made ill-considered loans.… A reformed IMF, working in conjunction with the World Bank and regional development banks, should ensure that foreign creditors are not bailed out while local population drown."[10]

The issue of fairness is not confined to those moments when the financial systems crash. It is an issue revealed by an examination of the economic data. Let us look at the data on the real income of American families from 1947 to 2005. During the first period from 1947 to 1976, the economy delivered dramatic improvements in the standard of living of most Americans: median real income more than doubled. By contrast, in the second period from 1976 to 2005, gains in living standards have been far less robust than they were during the previous period: median real income was only about 23 percent higher in 2005 than in 1976.[11]

The exhibit below shows that during the first half of the period covered, wage increase was at tandem with productivity. During the second period wage increase trailed behind productivity increase.

In comparison to ordinary workers, how have the top bankers fared? A report by New York attorney general's office released in July 2009 revealed that thousands of top traders and bankers on Wall Street were awarded huge bonuses and pay packages for 2008. And

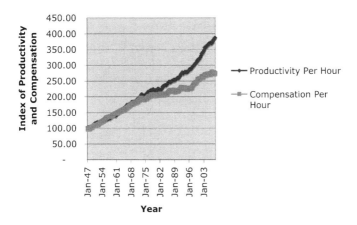

US non-farm business, productivity vs. compensation per hour, 1947–2008.[12]

this happened at a time when their banks recorded huge losses. Nine financial firms that received federal bailout money paid about 5,000 of their traders and bankers bonuses of more than $1 million each for 2008. Goldman Sachs paid million dollar-plus bonuses to 953 traders and bankers; Morgan Stanley granted similar payouts to 428 employees. Even weaker banks such as Citigroup and Bank of America distributed hundreds of million-dollar awards.[13]

The financial sector is not the only one that rewards top executives in spite of negative performance. One example outside the financial sector is provided by car-maker MG Rover. Its five executives took £42 million in pay and pensions even though the company was losing money and ran debts of more than £1 billion. The once famous company went into administration under insolvency procedures in April 2005; about 6,500 people lost their jobs.[14] The excessive pays enjoyed by the top executives is a glaring contrast to the pay of ordinary workers, which has remained stagnant in the background of rising productivity. It happened on the watch of former British Prime Minister Tony Blair. This makes the claim of a caring society so incredulous.

Another example of such unfair practice is the pay of CEOs. It is instructive to read a joint study by the Institute for Policy Studies and United for a Fair Economy, which was released in August 2007. The average CEO of a large US firm made roughly $10.8 million in 2006, or 364 times that of an American worker. The study also compared the American CEO pay to that of leaders in other fields and other countries. The top 20 highest-paid CEOs of public-held US companies earned an average of $36.4 million in 2006. That is 204 times that of the 20 highest paid US military generals, and 38 times that of the 20 highest paid leaders of non-profit organizations. They also made three times more than the top CEOs of European companies who had booked higher sales figures than their US counterparts. However, their high salaries are a pale comparison of what the top dogs in the private equity and hedge funds managers get. The average pay in 2006 of top 20 highest-earning private equity and hedge fund managers is $657.5 million. Number One on the list is James Simons of Renaissance Technologies, a hedge fund, who made $1.5 billion in 2006.[15]

It is useful to note that the huge pay packages enjoyed by American CEOs are not socially acceptable in many other countries. For example, Japan's biggest bank by capitalization paid a total of $8.1 million to its top 14 executives in the fiscal year ending 31 March 2008.

Japanese business emphasizes harmony among the staff over individual excellence. Seniority, rather than performance, is an important factor in determining pay.[16]

It is rather difficult to sustain the arguments for extremely high pay for top executives as the necessary price for their performance. First is the strange phenomenon of top bankers being bountifully rewarded when banks under their charge are spilling red ink. Second, it is very doubtful that lower but still generous pay cannot attract equally good or even better people to do the job. Third, top executives are severely overpaid because weak boards have allowed them to dictate the terms of their compensation. As a result, pay bears little relationship to performance and tends to rise inexorably. One prominent critic of the bonus orgies is Warren Buffett who attacked the system that lets chief executives choose the members of remuneration committees.[17] Corporate governance had degenerated from looking after stakeholder interests to shareholder interests. It has since slipped further down the slope to advancing the interests of senior executives at the expense of the company.

Attempts to legislate executive pay are not likely to be fruitful. The issue of pay lies within the domain of responsibility of the corporate board, i.e. it is an issue of corporate governance. Moreover, it is a reflection of social norms and values.

It Is a Matter of Social Legitimacy

In our times, one general rule is that people should be rewarded appropriately and fairly for their contribution. The crisis has prompted public interests in the excessive high pay enjoyed by top bankers. At the same time, it has also revealed that compensations for ordinary employees are too low relative to their contributions to productivity. This unfair treatment of workers has been going on for a few decades. Even Alan Greenspan is worried and he warns that "unless we begin to reverse a quarter century of increases in income inequality, the cultural ties that bind our society could become undone. Disaffection, breakdown of authority, even large-scale violence could ensue, jeopardizing the civility on which growing economies depend."[18]

Unfair pay is but one of the issues of social justice in the USA. Another is that major legislations from healthcare to financial reforms continue to be drafted in consultation with industrial lobbies.[19]

In the international arena, the USA fails to offer a shining example of acting fairly and generously. It is well known that the USA has been lagging behind other rich countries in making contributions to help the poor countries. What is worse, it has steered the IMF to behave in ways that hurt the victim countries of the Asian financial crisis.[20] To quote Joseph Stiglitz:

> It is now a commonplace that the international trade agreements about which the United States spoke so proudly only a few years ago were grossly unfair to countries in the third world. As I go to meetings of businessmen, whether in the rarefied seminars of Davos or the financial circles of New York or the high-tech world of Silicon Valley, practically all the people I see recognize the inequities and hypocrisies of American government policies.[21]

At a deeper level, we are talking about values, social norms, and culture. This is an essential point articulated by Ho Kwon Ping earlier on in the chapter. Its importance is admitted just as much by even the arch advocate of free market Alan Greenspan. He says;

> We cannot function without some set of values to guide the multitude of choices we make every day. The need for values is inbred. Their content is not. That need is driven by an innate moral sense in all of us, the basis upon which a majority have sought the guidance of the numerous religions that humans have embraced over the millennia. Part of that innate moral code is a sense of what is just and proper.[22]

That innate moral code or a sense of what is just and proper is more commonly known as a sense of fairness or social justice in human affairs. It is widely dispersed in diverse cultures and societies. The concept of social justice goes to the very heart of civilization. It is an index of the health of a society. We read accounts of this in history. One of the greatest challenges of the ruling group is to sell their version of fairness to the general population so that it becomes the accepted "rules of the game". Once accepted, it has the character of legitimacy. It can take the form of political legitimacy in the realm of politics, or social legitimacy in the realm of social affairs, and so on. It is a broader concept and more significant than the narrower concept of legality.

Interestingly, the concept of social legitimacy can be used to demystify some longstanding differences between the West and many Asian countries. For example, when the ruling party of China manages to lift hundreds of millions of the people out of extreme poverty, it can lay claim to social legitimacy. To most Chinese, the post-Mao leadership can justify its rule based on its performance. In China, social legitimacy has acted as the basis for political legitimacy. However, in the USA, political legitimacy has been used to ignore the issue of social legitimacy. The issue of employees' pay increase lagging behind productivity increase is a serious matter because it goes against the grain and core values of liberal capitalism. In the end, hanky-panky affairs of Wall Street and grave income disparities have the potential to undermine the legitimacy of capitalism as a system.

The following passage from an article by Felix Rohatyn[a] in *The New York Review of Books* sums up the sad situation well.[23]

> The most important economic issue facing the US today is the issue of fairness. The stock market boom and its inevitable bust have created ever-wider gaps between the very wealthy and the rest of Americans. The outrageous compensation packages of many corporate managers and the abuses that have been exposed throughout our financial institutions have shaken the public's faith in the fairness of the American system. It has convinced overseas critics that American-style capitalism and globalization exploit the less fortunate. It may convince many Americans of the same thing.

---

[a] A former US Ambassador to France, he is an investment banker best known for his role in rescuing the New York City from bankruptcy in the 1970s.

Rohatyn clarifies that though he believes that market capitalism is the best economic system ever invented for the creation of wealth, it must be fair, it must be regulated, and it must be ethical. He goes on to warn that:

> Only capitalists can kill capitalism, but the system cannot stand much more abuse of the type we have witnessed recently. Such companies as Enron, WorldCom, Global Crossing, and Tyco, and their CEOs, cannot be allowed to be representative of American business. These corporate leaders were high-level thieves who stole from their shareholders and employees to enrich themselves. It will take a while to absorb just how brazenly they violated the law and betrayed their responsibilities. Unless corporate leaders can demonstrate their commitment to fairness and respect for law, the future of American capitalism will be in jeopardy.

Though published in November 2002, the passages read as if they were published in the aftermath of the 2008 crisis. It is difficult to avoid having a feeling of *déjà vu*. Perhaps the political elites have not seen the rot as serious or they have simply ignored it. Or there is a lack of political will and leadership to reform it.

The same article carries a message that is very relevant for political leaders.

> A political leader can ask for considerable sacrifice from the American public if the sacrifice is seen as justified and is distributed reasonably fairly. I doubt that the public feels such fairness exists today in view

of tax cuts heavily weighted in favor of upper-income Americans, as well as the disclosures of corporate scandals in which senior executives walked away with hundreds of millions of dollars while employees lost their jobs and their savings.[24]

Economic Development as Part of Societal Development

As early as 2,300 years ago, the Greek philosophers Plato and Aristotle insisted that economic development should be embedded in social development.[25] The role of economic activity is to promote the well-being of the citizens of the ideal city state, of a just and harmonious community. Currently, the opposite of this position is happening in almost every corner of the earth. Economic development is seen to be more important than social development. Grow the GNP and let us hope that social problems would disappear mysteriously. The emphasis is on the economy. An alternative approach, in line with the thinking of Plato and Aristotle, would be social harmony, pleasant living and working environment, environmental protection, and cultural and intellectual advancements. The emphasis is on the social dimension, and this should be used to guide economic policies.

It is important to note that this ancient Greek tradition was very much alive in the works of great economists such as Adam Smith (1723–1790), John Stuart Mill (1806–1873), Alfred Marshall (1842–1924), and Arthur Pigou (1877–1959).[26] While they worked to uncover the mechanism of creating economic wealth, they never neglected the issue of social welfare and role of the state in dealing with market failures. Writing in the midst of the financial crisis, Amartya Sen reminds his readers that Adam Smith was deeply concerned with moral issues and social justice. This aspect was quite evident in Smith's various writings in which he expressed his deep concern about the fate of the poor and the disadvantaged. Moreover, he was conscious of the limitations of the market.

> The most immediate failure of the market mechanism lies in the things that the market leaves *undone*. Smith's economic analysis went well beyond leaving everything to the invisible hand of the market mechanism. He was not only a defender of the role of the state in providing public services, such as education, and in poverty relief … he was also deeply concerned about the inequality and poverty that might survive in an otherwise successful market economy... it would also be hard to carve out from his works any theory arguing for the sufficiency of market forces, or of the need to accept the dominance of capital.[27]

Adam Smith's *The Wealth of Nations* is better known than his earlier work *The Theory of Moral Sentiments*. But the two books must be read together. In *The Theory*. Smith examined the strong need for actions based on values that go well beyond profit seeking.[28] While he wrote that "prudence" was "of all the virtues that which is most useful to the individual", he insisted that "humanity, justice, generosity, and public spirit, are the qualities most useful to others."[29]

Smith believed that honest people, if allowed to pursue their own interests, would fare better than they would under a system that dictated what was "good". In so doing, persons pursuing their own interests would reduce inefficiencies and allocate resources where they would benefit the greater society. Somehow, the role of self-interests has led to the interpretation that Smith rejected state intervention. This is an unfortunate misconception. He rejected only state interventions that exclude the market, but not interventions that include the market while aiming to do those important things that the market may leave undone.[30]

Another great economist who continued the tradition of not losing sight of social welfare while creating economic wealth is John Stuart Mill.[31] He did not believe that one's interests and others' need to be mutually exclusive. Put differently, he believed that an increase in personal pleasure can also be derived from participation in the happiness of others. In this way, he justified from a utilitarian perspective the rationality of behavior motivated by feelings of humanity and solidarity. He allowed for departure from *laissez faire* principle. He accepted the principle of state intervention in the economy in the regulation of working day, and assistance to the poor. Though he supported private property and the rights of individuals to possess the products of their own labor, he criticized the abuses of such rights, especially the glaring inequality in wealth distribution. The idea was to bring about a compromise between the baser and the higher pursuits of man.

Mill's ideas were further developed by Alfred Marshall, who was initiator of the tendency that tried to reconcile a moderate *laissez faire* with a reformist program.[32] Like Mill, he rejected the view that the only way to improve the conditions of the poor was to stimulate the egoism of the rich. There was an inextricable interweaving among the economic, social, and cultural spheres of human activity, and a strong link between material and moral facts. It was a link that had implications for the role of the state. Marshall believed that the social-political dimension of human action should always be taken into account by economists. This formed the conceptual and moral basis for state intervention. The state had the right and duty to intervene in the economic sphere, to regulate the market mechanism and to correct its distortions. The argument was explicitly and strongly expressed in *The Social Possibilities of Economic Chivalry* (1907). He advocated the introduction of corrective mechanisms such as cooperative movements, profit-sharing, arbitration on wages, and similar mechanisms into the English political economic system. His thinking laid the foundation of welfare economics. The study of economic welfare must include the study of situations of market failures, i.e. when market mechanism failed to produce the beneficial effects.

Marshall's study of social welfare was continued by Arthur Pigou who succeeded him as professor of economics at Cambridge University. Pigou's major work, *The Economics of Welfare* (1920), brought welfare economics into the scope of economic analysis. In particular, he was responsible for the distinction between private and social marginal products and costs. He originated the idea that governments could, via a mixture of taxes and subsidies, correct market failures. To honor his contribution in this area, the term *Pigovian taxes* was coined to mean taxes used to correct negative externalities.[33]

Pigou was a contemporary of John Keynes. And like Keynes, Pigou was very concerned with the psychological basis of recession. However, he paid more attention to the problems of unequal distribution of wealth, and he also pioneered the use of economic inequality as a key indicator for economic assessment and policy. He is certainly very relevant today.

Luckily, the spirits and teachings of the great economists discussed above have not left the economic profession and can be found in the works of Jeffery Sachs, Amartya Sen, Joseph Stiglitz, and their soul mates.[34] For years, they have been arguing that the rich countries ought to treat the poor countries more fairly. In times like this, the rich countries must increase their assistance to help the poor countries, which suffer from a problem not of their own making. The contribution is all the more necessary and urgent in view of the fact that the crisis could push 53 million more people into extreme poverty, according to an estimate by the World Bank.[35]

The Slide from Liberalism to Neoliberalism

We have come a long way from the days of liberalism so powerfully articulated by Adam Smith and his intellectual descendants. Liberalism has morphed into neoliberalism that has appropriated the symbols and language of liberalism but goes against its humanitarian values. To the neoliberals, a state should restrict itself to the protection of property rights and the defence of the nation and to the administration of justice based on individual rights. The state does not concern itself with the issue of economic production and distribution. That is left to the markets. Markets are the economic institutions that can best play the role in facilitating the production and circulation of wealth. State involvement in the matter can only result in an outcome that is inferior to that accruing from unregulated self-seeking capitalists. State taxation needed for state fiscal policy has been attacked by neoliberal Robert Nozick as forced labor.[36]

As pointed out by Michael Sandel,[b] under the influence of neoliberal thinking, the market has vastly expanded its roles and has taken over some vital functions of the state. Social critics have been voicing their worries that private corporations, by their very nature, are not the best agencies to act as provider of public services. The financial meltdown offers them another platform to launch their attack.

> The slide from liberal to neoliberal thinking occurs in every domain of economic discourse, and it is especially clear in banking. Banks are institutions, chartered by public authority, to serve public purpose. The state has power over the conduct of banks, including taking them over and running them when they are troubled enough to threaten the public guarantee that lies behind bank deposits. 'Financial markets' and

---

[b] See Chapter 2.

especially the 'shadow banking system' are neoliberal creations that escape both regulation and insurance. The result has been to vitiate the concept of public purpose, creating in banks privileged and powerful market-oriented institutions that use and largely control the state, rather than respond to it...[37]

Hopeful Signs of Change

Lest we fall prey to a bout of pessimism, there is a sign of change for the better. *The Economist* (6 June 2009) carries a piece of interesting news. At an unofficial ceremony on 3 June 2009, the day before their graduation, more than 400 Harvard MBA students took a special oath. They promised they would serve the greater good, act with the utmost integrity and guard against "decisions and behaviour that advance my own narrow ambitions, but harm the enterprise and the societies it serves". These students want to distance themselves from earlier generations of MBAs, who were seen to have contributed to the turmoil, especially on Wall Street, the biggest employer of Harvard MBAs in recent years. They believe that the goal of maximizing shareholder value has become a justification for short-termism and, in particular, rapid personal enrichment. "They are concerned about managers doing things that drive up the share price quickly at the expense of a firm's lasting health."[38] It is too early to say whether the students' change of heart heralds a cultural shift in the business world or it is just a change that will die away as a ripple.

However, it is good to listen to a verse in the movie *The Sound of Music*: "Nothing comes from nothing, nothing ever will." Management gurus such as Jim Collins argue that shareholders are likely to earn better returns in the long run if firms are led by managers with integrity and a desire to play a constructive role in society.[39] Besides the issue of integrity, it is worth bearing in mind this basic principle: companies operate with the consent of society; they serve the needs of customers and society and earn a profit based on that. If they can remain true to their oaths, the new Harvard MBAs would show how societal interests, firms' profits and their own future have a symbiotic relationship.

Endnotes

1. *Source*: http://www.cowboylyrics.com/lyrics/rich-john/shuttin-detroit-down-26813html [accessed on 20 September 2009].

2. Michael Lim Mah Hui and Lim Chin (2010). *Nowhere to Hide,* Singapore: ISEAS.

3. John F Burns and Landon Thomas Jr (2009). Anglo-American Capitalism on Trial, *The New York Times*, 28 March 2009 [accessed on 20 September 2009]. Available at http://www.nytimes.com/2009/03/29/weekinreview/29burns.html.

4. IMF Says World in Recession, Auto Giants Flop [accessed on 21 October 2009]. Available at http://sg.news.yahoo.com/afp/20090422/tts-finance-economy-world-c1b2fc3.html.

5. Robert M Solow (2009). How to Understand Disaster, *The New York Review of Books*, 56(8), May 14.

   Richard A Posner (2009). *A Failure of Capitalism: The Crisis of '08 and the Descent into Depression, Cambridge and London*: Harvard University Press.

6. Michael Sandel (2009). Markets and Morals, Lecture One of BBC 2009 Reith Lecture [accessed on 15 August 2009]. Available at http://www.bbc.co.uk/programmes/b00729d9.

7. Ho Kwon Ping (2009). Developing an East Asian Business Ethos, in *Destructive Creativity of Wall Street and the East Asian Response*, Michael Heng Siam-Heng and Lim Tai Wei (eds.) Singapore: World Scientific, pp. 222–223.

8. John Eatwell and Lance Taylor (2000). *Global Finance at Risk,* New York: New Press.

9. Alan S Blinder (1999). Eight Steps to a New Financial Order, *Foreign Affairs*, 78(5), pp. 50–63.

10. Alan S Blinder (1999).

11. Paul Krugman (2007). Who Was Milton Friedman? *The New York Review of Books*, 54(2), 15 February.

12. Michael Lim Mah Hui and Lim Chin (2010).

13. Executive Pay, *The New York Times*, 14 October 2009, [accessed 20 September 2009]. Available at http://topics. nytimes.com/top/reference/timestopics/subjects/e/executive_pay/index.html.

14. Rover Bosses Took £42m from Firm, *BBC news*, 10 September 2009. [accessed on 20 September 2009]. Available at http://news.bbc.co.uk/go/pr/fr/-/2/hi/business/8248923.stm.

15. Executive Excesses 2007 — the Staggering Social Cost of US Business Leadership [accessed on 20 September

2009]. Available at http://www.ips-dc.org/reports/070829-executiveexcess.pdf.

16. Yuka Hayashi and Phred Dvorak (2008). Japanese Wrestle with CEO Pay as They Go Global, *The Wall Street Journal*, 28 November, [accessed on 1 December 2008]. Available at http://online.wsj.com/article/SB122782362228562381.html.

17. Attacking the Corporate Gravy Train, *The Economist*, 30 May 2009.

18. Alan Greenspan (2007). *The Age of Turbulence*, New York: The Penguin Press, p. 468.

19. Financial and monetary issues as the crisis unfolds, Public Policy Brief, Highlights No. 103A, 2009, The Levy Economics Institute of Bard College.

20. Alan S Blinder (1999).

21. Joseph E Stiglitz (2002). A Fair Deal for the World, *New York Review of Books*, 49(9), 23 May.

22. Alan Greenspan (2007). p. 17.

23. Felix G Rohatyn (2002). From New York to Baghdad, The New York Review of Books, 49(18), 21 November.

24. Felix G Rohatyn (2002).

25. Ching-Yao Hsieh and Meng Hua Ye (1991). *Economics, Philosophy, and Physics*, Armonk, N.Y.: M.E. Sharpe.

   Gunarti Endro (2007). Integrity in economic life: an Aristotelian perspective, Singapore: unpublished PhD thesis, Department of Philosophy, National University of Singapore.

26. Ernesto Screpanti and Stefano Zamagni (1995). *An Outline of the History of Economic Thought*, Oxford: Clarendon Press.

   Eric Roll (1992). *A History of Economic Thought*, London: Faber and Faber.

27. Amartya Sen (2009). Capitalism beyond the Crisis, *New York Review of Books*, 26 March.

28. Amartya Sen (2009).

29. Amartya Sen (2009). The quote is from Adam Smith (1976). *The Theory of Moral Sentiments*, DD Raphael and AL Macfie (eds.) Oxford: Clarendon Press, pp. 189–190.

30. Amartya Sen (2009).

31. Ernesto Screpanti and Stefano Zamagni (1995).
        Eric Roll (1992).

32. Ernesto Screpanti and Stefano Zamagni (1995).
        Eric Roll (1992).

33. Arthur Cecil Pigou, Wikipedia [accessed on 7 December 2009]. Available at http://en.wikipedia.org/wiki/Arthur_Cecil_Pigou#Academic_work.
        Ernesto Screpanti and Stefano Zamagni (1995).
        Eric Roll (1992).

34. Details about them can be found in Wikipedia.

35. Forgotten Sibling *The Economist*, 25 April 2009, p. 73.

36. Robert Nozick (1974). *Anarchy, State and Utopia*, New York: Basic Books.

37. Financial and monetary issues as the crisis unfolds, Public Policy Brief, Highlights No. 103A, 2009, The Levy Economics Institute of Bard College.

38. Forswearing Greed, *The Economist*, 6 June 2009.

39. ibid.

Chapter Eight

A New Financial Landscape?

> A system — any system, economic or other — that at
> *every* point of time fully utilizes its possibilities to the
> best advantage may yet in the long run be inferior to a
> system that does so at *no* given point of time, because
> the latter's failure to do so may be a condition for the
> level or speed of a long run performance.
>
> — Joseph Schumpeter[1]

Introduction

As a result of the current financial crisis, there have been
calls to do something to reduce the frequency of financial
crisis as well as the scale and scope of its impact. There
is general consensus that the whole financial sector has to
be better regulated. But what we have seen so far are only
half-hearted reforms. They would not reduce the size of
the over-grown sector. There is no proposal to break up
giant financial firms with numerous messy inter-
connections with other financial firms. Absurd derivatives such as naked CDSs are not banned.

One positive outcome of the crisis is the consensus
that central banks must not only control inflation, but

they must also look after broader financial stability, and to curb asset bubble.

Against this timid reform, this chapter outlines the structure of a simpler financial system to serve as a fail-safe payment system, a custodian of savings and as a financial intermediary to promote productive and useful investment. It eschews high finance and complex products. Given the critical importance of finance in economic development, countries that have robust and sound financial systems enjoy a competitive edge.

Prospects of Meaningful Reforms

Exactly one year after the demise of Lehman Brothers, President Obama used the anniversary to deliver a tough message to Wall Street. "The old ways that led to this crisis cannot stand," he said. "History cannot be allowed to repeat itself." He also called on the US Congress to act on regulatory reforms he hailed as the most sweeping bid to tame irrational exuberance since the Great Depression. While conceding that much of the blame should fall on the USA, he urged other global powers to do more to rein in financial industry abuses. "The financial crisis created a once-in-a-generation opportunity to modernize our outdated financial regulatory system," he added.[2]

There are good reasons why Obama sounded so stern. Several days before his speech, Morgan Stanley promised its employees so much pay in the third quarter that it almost made an underlying loss. That happened in spite of months of public outcry against the way banks pay their own staff at the expense of their shareholders. Moreover, banks rely on taxpayers' support, which is huge. Loans from central banks and debt guarantees alone amount to $2.7 trillion. Another worrying point is that investment banks have not lowered their risk appetite. Based on statistical measures of the maximum trading losses on risk-adjusted assets, the nine biggest investment banks are taking more risk. Their combined balance-sheet is 40 percent bigger in September 2009 than in mid-2005.[3] It is obvious that neither moral persuasion nor public outcry is going to work.

The crisis has passed. But will America emerge with a far sounder financial system? Should we take the good President for his words and expect a radically reformed financial system — a sound and robust system that reduces speculation to the minimum, a system that channels idle money to economically productive and socially useful investment?

Let us try to take a look at the proposed changes as presented by Treasury Secretary Timothy Geithner in the House Financial Services Committee hearing on 23 September 2009. The important points are:

1. All financial firms are required to hold higher capital and liquidity buffers. The requirements are higher for the largest, most leveraged, and most interconnected firms that pose the greatest risk to the system as a whole.

2. Those big interconnected firms have to prepare plans detailing how they should be dismantled in the event of failure. They will provide for the orderly unwinding of these firms that protects taxpayers and the broader economy while ensuring that losses are borne by creditors and other stakeholders.

3. The Consumer Financial Protection Agency is to be set up to protect consumers and to provide rules on sustainable innovation.

4. Over-the-counter derivative markets are to be regulated. It includes substantially increasing the use of central clearing platforms. It will include strengthening supervision and regulation of critical payment, clearing, and settlement systems.

To the many who have hoped for a more radical reform, the proposals are certainly a disappointment. To be fair, there are some welcome proposals, and this is to be expected given the gravity of the crisis. Increase of capital requirement as contained in Point One is a positive one; it is an effective way to reduce leverage by financial firms.

Point Two is essentially the "living wills," which is intended to send a message that big banks are not likely to be rescued because of their size. But it still allows big conglomerate banks to operate. History has time and again shown that financial firms somehow fail to exercise internal discipline in boom times. They are prone to indulge in activities that produce super-profits, even at tremendous risks to their own survival. Their creditors and shareholders have displayed minimal ability to effectively check and control such tricky practices. The living wills construction, if successfully implemented, may deal partially with the issue of moral hazards, but by itself it does not deal with the problem of systemic risks due to failures of big banks. It is like telling reckless drivers that there will be no ambulance to help them if they crash. This may reduce the number of accidents but it does not outlaw reckless driving. We have to assume that there will always be reckless drivers. It makes more sense to ban reckless driving.

"Too big to fail" financial institutions must be broken up into small ones. Some of them even after being broken up will still continue their reckless practices. However, the damage caused by small banks is not systemic, unlike those caused by those "too big to fail" banks with their web of connections. In fact the rationales for big banks have come under scrutiny, even by bankers themselves. "Admittedly there are some benefits from size. But the empirical evidence suggests that these benefits are rather limited," said Philip Hildebrand, vice chairman of the Swiss National Bank's governing board.[4] Moreover, many big banks have become too difficult to run. Even HSBC, a bank well known for its prudence and a history of astute acquisitions, has stumbled in recent years when entering markets where unfamiliarity prevented it from bringing these traits to bear.[5]

The principle behind breaking big banks is to protect the interests of the public and banks' business clients, while that behind living wills is to appeal to the self-interests of big banks to look after themselves. Time and again, the latter principle has failed to work for bankers who are focused on lining their own pockets.

Point Three on protection of consumers by setting up an agency similar to Food and Drug Administration is a good idea. However, it is disturbing that investment banks are concocting another kind of product pretty similar to subprime securitization. Instead of mortgage, it is life insurance derivatives.[6] The banks plan to buy life insurance policies that ill and elderly people sell for cash.

Then, they securitize these policies, packaging the insurance policies together into bonds, to be sold to investors who will receive the payouts when people with the insurance die.

Point Four suggests that the proposed measures to deal with financial weapons of mass destruction do not match the strong words used. Absurd derivatives such as naked CDS are not banned. Does it suggest that attempts to reform the CDS market have been met with fierce opposition by Wall Street, and the White House and the legislators have to backtrack?

In short, critics will see the proposed measures as not effective. The proposals seem to confirm a recurring pattern. The world has gone through numerous financial crises since the Great Depression. In the wake of every major crisis, there are calls for reforming the financial systems to make them more stable and robust. But when the economy recovers and as memory of the dark days fade, it is again back to business as usual. Of course, because of the gravity of the current crisis, there are some attempts to roll back deregulation. But these changes do not touch the core of the matter. As the French are fond of saying, "Plus ça change, plus c'est la même chose."[a]

Rightly or wrongly, the response of the political elites in the USA seems to reaffirm the feeling that "Wall Street, after getting billions of taxpayer dollars, will emerge from the financial crisis looking much the same as before markets collapsed."[7] The reasons were pointed

---

[a] A French aphorism which means, "The more things change, the more they remain the same."

out by Simon Johnson, former chief economist of the IMF: "Throughout the crisis, the government has taken extreme care not to upset the interests of the financial institutions, or to question the basic outlines of the system that got us here," and the elite business interests that played a central role in creating the crisis are now using their influence to prevent precisely the sorts of reforms that are needed.[8]

The Financial Sector Is Far Too Big

Another blind spot in the proposed reform is that there is no plan to trim down the oversized financial sector. The point that the financial sector is too big is succinctly stated by Paul Krugman:

> We went from an economy in which about 4 percent of GDP came from the financial sector to an economy in which 8 percent of GDP come from the financial sector, and in which at its peak 41 percent of profits were being earned by the financial sector. And there is no reason to believe that anything productive happened as a result of all of that. These extremely highly compensated bankers were essentially just finding new ways to offload risks on to other people.[9]

Expressing a similar view, another economist, Willem Buiter of the London School of Economics, argues that a stripped-down sort of finance could do most of what a modern economy needs.[10]

It is almost commonsensical to say that the financial system is part of the economic system, and that financial services need to be adapted to serve the economy. In so far as it makes the *real* economy operate more efficiently, it does have a useful function to perform. Its primary role as a financial intermediary is to collect people's savings and make them available to those who can direct them into productive and useful investment and activities. Along the way, it also spreads risks to and rewards those who *are able and willing* to bear them. "When it goes much beyond that, the financial system is likely to cause more trouble than it averts," says Robert Solow.[11] One fact suggests strongly that the financial sector is not positively engaged in allocating financial resources. As of 2007, players in the financial market traded roughly $300 worth of stocks and bonds for every dollar that non-financial corporations raise for new investments in plant and equipment. This ratio is about three times what it was only a decade ago, at the peak of the dot-com bubble.[12] It has more to do with speculation and far too little to do with channeling money for investment.

Overgrown and bloated financial sector has a sociocultural dimension as well as political dimension too. The sociocultural dimension may be expressed in the words of John Kay.

> ... we need to have markets in stocks, bonds, foreign currencies, even derivatives: but what we need is only a small fraction of the volume of trading in them which takes place. In inclusive societies, the main restraint on the growth of these activities is simply that they do not command very much respect. In individualistic societies this sanction has declined, and we are even encouraged to believe that what is profitable

is demonstrated to be valuable by that fact alone. But it is quite difficult to justify market economies as a means of creating wealth when the largest rewards so obviously go to those who trade in existing assets.[13]

Assuming a moral high ground, one commentator interprets the large share of the financial industry in the US economy as a sign of decadence of the society.[14]

Politically, the financial sector has exercised a disproportionate influence over the body politic of America. Highly paid bankers have become important contributors of funds for political campaigns. With the financial sector becoming increasingly bloated its political clout also grew.[15] At the same time, senior executives of Wall Street serve as top officials in the US government while well-placed officials obtain lucrative jobs at Wall Street firms after they leave government office.[16]

New Roles for Central Banks

For past decades, it was the consensus that the prime task of central banks was to keep inflation low and stable. Price stability reduces uncertainty and allows households and business firms to plan ahead. Though there were debates about the responsibility of central banks to curb assets inflation, there was no consensus. Some central bankers in Europe and Japan held that monetary policy should "lean against" asset bubbles. US Fed officials said that bubbles were hard to spot, and argued that it was less costly to clean up by cutting rates after they burst.

The crisis has brought to the fore the duty of central bankers for broader financial stability. That is the broad consensus reached at their meeting in Jackson Hole, the USA, in August 2009. In many countries, there are plans to give them responsibility to curb financial excesses.

Central banks such as the Fed have to control asset prices in order to prevent asset bubbles because they are so frequent.[17] It is now more widely accepted that rates might also need to rise to stem an asset bubble.[18] Another measure is to impose a tax such as stamp duty on stock transaction.[19] The tax can be increased in boom time to discourage speculation.

We Need Boring Financial Systems

One of the lessons of the crisis is that high finance with complex products has proved to be destructive to economy and to the banks that embrace it. Put differently, banks that stick to simple products and services have thrived well. One such bank is the Erste Bank, a big retail bank in Austria. Its chairman, Mr. Andreas Treichl, believes that commercial banks should keep their strategies simple and their ambitions relatively modest. "We should not think we can invent something brilliant. If we could we would be working somewhere else," he says of the exotic credit derivatives that spread risk, like a contagion, through the financial system.[20] The Erste Bank is a good illustration of the virtues of a boring bank. In fact, more than boring banks, we need a boring financial system. This point is highlighted by Paul Krugman. He says:

> In the aftermath of the Great Depression, we redesigned the machine so that we *did* understand it, well enough at any rate to avoid big disasters. Banks,

the piece of the system that malfunctioned so badly in the 1930s, were placed under tight regulation and supported by a strong safety net. Meanwhile, international movements of capital, which played a disruptive role in the 1930s, were also limited. The financial system became a little boring but much safer.[21]

With the benefits of so many crises behind us, it is not difficult to see how things have gone astray. The details and specifics may differ, but the important lesson is that financial crises tend to erupt violently when we ignore the basics. Assuming that governments follow responsible macroeconomic policies, what are the important features of a sound and robust financial system? It is submitted that it must perform the followings:

- Efficient allocation of money for proper consumption and productive investment.
- The payment system must be robust enough to function properly even during financial crises.
- Credit is available to firms so that they can conduct their businesses without disruption.
- Risk is spreading evenly and broadly to those who are able and willing to bear it and without increasing the risk for the system. This is consistent with the position that the best way to safeguard the real economy while protecting the public purse is to ensure that essential financial services to individuals and businesses are regulated and that banks abstain from undue risk-taking.[22]
- Any financial institution that is too big to fail is broken up into smaller institutions.

The proposed financial system is a three-tiered system. The first tier is a banking and payment sub-system that is made up of banks and they run in a conservative manner, like the post bank of the past. The regulation here is very tight.

The second tier is made up of insurance firms and commercial banks where the regulation ranges from tight to moderate. They are allowed to indulge in low-risk to moderately risky business. They are required to build up their resources during good times in order to meet their obligations during bad times, based on time honored actuarial practices. In times of financial crisis, the state may bail them out by buying their assets if they are likely to survive in ordinary time.

The third tier consists of other financial firms such as private banks, merchant banks, and investment banks. Though they are the least regulated of the three categories of financial firms, they are still subjected to the criteria of transparency and spreading their risks. They are not allowed to assume risks that are beyond their capacity to bear. In times of financial crisis, they cannot expect help from the state.

Payment and Custodian System Consisting of Narrow Banks

The core of the payment and custodian system is made up of banks that operate pretty much like post banks of the good old days. In other words, they are the banks with a narrow focus. All the deposits are fully guaranteed by the state. Savers earn low interest while credits are given to very low-risk clients. The interest margin is the source of their operational expenses and profit. The core banks are all local banks, i.e. with no overseas branches. They have branches all over the country, housed in modest premises. To cut cost, they rely a lot on Internet and telephone banking to run their operations.

Their customers are likely to be government agencies, schools, non-profit organizations, and risk-averse individuals. Business firms would also have accounts with the banks for the purpose of using them as payment system as well as safe custodian of their money.

The key concepts are efficiency, robustness, and fail-safe. The analogy is like running a telephone system that has to be in the air all the time. Shareholders of these banks are forewarned that they cannot expect their investment to earn huge profits. In the same vein, board of directors and senior managers are selected based on their commitment to public service, integrity, and prudence.

The core banks serve as safe havens for depositors in times of financial turmoil. Bank runs take the form of withdrawals from weak banks to be redeposited in the core banks. The level of aggregate bank reserves is thus maintained. In such a situation, runs on weak banks will not produce instability in the banking system.[23] This ensures that the credit and payment system can continue to function uninterrupted.

Though the system of core banks would function as the robust payment system, they are not able to meet the needs of business firms and those with more complex financial needs. For that we need insurance companies and commercial banks.

Insurance Companies and Commercial Banks

Insurance companies have built up a body of knowledge that has withstood the test of time. The time horizon is long. They have lots of historical data as well as actuarial science to help them decide the premium to be charged for a certain policy. As long as they exercise prudence, eschew undue risk taking, and use financial engineering instruments appropriately, they are most unlikely to get into trouble. The case of AIG illustrates vividly what can go wrong when a small department wrote enough derivatives contracts to nearly sink this otherwise well-managed giant firm.

Insurance companies have an important role in the social and economic life. For example, airlines cannot fly their plane unless the plane is insured. You cannot drive your car on the road unless it has insurance cover. Insurance firms are privileged in the sense that such legal requirements create a big and stable market for their products and services. They also act like pension funds when they sell life insurance to customers. If they sell health insurance, then they act effectively as part of the national health services. For all these reasons, insurance firms are to operate under strict supervision.

Like insurance companies, commercial banks too have a long history of experience to guide their business operations. They take deposits from their customers and lend out the money to creditworthy clients. The state guarantees up to a certain amount of the deposits. In return for this privilege, the commercial banks are regulated, though not as tightly as the core banks.

During the boom period, the central bank requires the banks to increase their provision in case of loan defaults — a kind of countercyclical measure. They are not allowed to set up off-balance-sheet Special Investment Vehicle to bypass regulations.

If somehow a commercial bank takes excessive risk and is going bust in bad times, it cannot expect a bailout from the state. All that the state can do is to refund the guaranteed quantum of money to depositors without any interest, advise them to transfer the money to the core banks and let the errant bank disappear. This is to reduce the ever recurrent problems associated with moral hazards.

Other Financial Firms

Under this rubric will fall merchant banks, private banks, investment banks, hedge funds, and venture capital firms. They are not allowed to take deposits. Though they are not so tightly regulated, it does not mean that they can do what they like. They still have to abide by general regulations of running a business. That includes being forbidden to trade in products that are too complex or against the principles of moral and social responsibility. "Financial products that have attributes of insurance have to be treated as insurance products and regulated accordingly."[24] In other words, CDSs will be regulated like any other insurance products.

These financial firms are the most innovative, and have a penchant for risk taking. They are the avid seekers of opportunities and if they get it right, they are well rewarded. What if they get it wrong? Bank regulation and supervision are intended not to stop them from making mistakes, but to make sure that if they get into a nasty mess, they do not hurt the innocent parties and cause a meltdown of the financial system. To this end, they are allowed to take risks to the extent that they can bear the full cost of the risks themselves.[25] They are not allowed to make inflated claims. They are also required to make very explicit to their clients the perils they are courting when they buy certain products and services.

They run their business like any other businesses. The fate of the business is mainly in the hands of their shareholders and the managers appointed by them. Buyers of their bonds are also forewarned that they do face the danger of loan default just like they buy any other commercial papers.

These firms will not expect bailout or any other forms of state assistance in times of difficulties. However, the state can help by way of working closing with the financial market to set up clearing house so that no specific firm is caught with too much obligations on its books.

Merits of the Proposed Setup

The proposed financial system ensures that the payment system continues to operate in time of financial crises. This serves as the most basic infrastructure of the financial system. It is like other utilities. The business is boring but it is crucially important. It is unlikely to attract people who enjoy tackling new problems at the job.

There is little room for innovation except in the area of efficiency enhancement and improvement of what the staff knows well.

However, the system has room for some initiative and innovation. They are to be found in insurance firms and commercial banks. These firms operate on time-honored principles and practices. As along as they are prudent and exercise due diligence, they are going to earn an honest living while rendering a vital service to the economic well being of society.

For the risk takers and advantage seekers, there is the sector of merchant banks and investment banks, private banks and venture capital firms. Here one is able to exercise one's talent in coming up with new products and services. It does not mean, however, it is free for all, without any supervision at all. The supervision is restricted to prevention of systemic meltdown of the financial system and cheating the innocent and ignorant.

International Financial Architecture

Beyond the operations of the financial system of an individual country, we have the operations of financial systems of various countries interacting with each other, understood broadly under the term international financial architecture. The financial world has undergone tremendous changes since the Bretton Woods agreements in 1944. An important milestone was the breakdown of the Bretton Woods system in 1971. Since then, there have been calls to reform and upgrade the system to meet the demands of the new circumstances. Suffice it to mention two examples — the Mexico financial crisis and the Asian financial crisis.

Reflecting on the financial crisis of Mexico, which erupted in 1994, Lawrence Summers writes:

> The IMF's present surveillance efforts, and indeed the analyses that go on in many of the world's finance ministries, were appropriate for the current-account-centred world of 20 years ago. They are not sufficient for today's more capital-account-centred world. Rather, to be useful today, analyses must focus more attention on the composition of capital flows, the risks of liquidity problems, and the possible reaction of capital markets to political shocks. The style as well as the substance of surveillance exercises needs to be changed. The once-a-year cycle of sending teams of analysts to interview national officials and examine the books may have fit the rhythms of earlier eras. It is not appropriate today.... The international community must develop a greater capacity to respond to financial emergencies.[26]

In the aftermath of the Asian financial crisis a decade ago, there was again some very serious rethinking of the structure of the international financial system.[27] It forms part of the continuing talks about reshaping the global financial system into a robust, stable, and resilient system.[28] The prescriptions imposed by the IMF were broadly seen to favor foreign creditor banks at the expense of the poor in those countries hit by the crisis. The prestige of the Fund took a dive. There was attempt to set up an Asian Monetary Fund, though it was in the end thwarted by Washington.

As it had so often happened in the past, the enthusiasm for strengthening the system faded into the background when the turmoil blew over. But with the biggest crisis of our lifetime looming large, the fervor for reform has returned. There has been an active debate in the mass media, financial circles, governments, and research community on the issues of free flow of capital, reforming the IMF, international reserve currencies, and maintenance of huge foreign reserves as defensive measure against speculative currency attacks.[29]

Conclusion

Based on the impact of the crisis on American economy and society and its global standing, Wall Street has wreaked more damage to the body politic of the country, its economy, and society beyond the fondest dreams of America's worst enemy.

Those countries that are able to tame the financial sector are going to have an edge in the global competition. The crisis has provided ample experiences to give us an outline of some of the important elements of what a robust financial system should possess.

Central banks must do their best to channel savings toward productive investment and away from speculative. In the institutional sense, countries more capable of carrying out this task have a competitive edge. This is especially so in the long run.

It has often been observed that investors and speculators behave very much like gamblers in casinos. And like casinos, financial markets must be strictly regulated. Visitors to casinos can and do often lose their shirts. No casino operator would extend a credit line to gamblers. Their losses are just limited to what they own and the adverse consequences affect only their families. The economy and society are not affected.

Endnotes

1. Joseph A Schumpeter (1942). *Capitalism, Socialism and Democracy*, p. 83. New York: Harper and Brothers.
2. Obama lashes out at Wall Street, AFP News, 15 September 2009 [accessed on 16 September 2009] Available at http://sg.news.yahoo.com/afp/20090914/tts-us-finance-economy-obama-972e412.html.
3. Unnatural Selection, The Economist. 12 September 2009.
4. "Too Big to Fail" Must Be Tackled Swiftly: Central Banker [accessed on 19 November 2009] Available at http://sg.news.yahoo.com/afp/20091119/tts-finance-banking-bank-switzerland-c1b2fc3.html.
5. Dummies for Finance, *The Economist*, 5 September 2009.
6. Marshall Auerback and Randall Wray (2009). Banks running wild: the subversion of insurance by "life settlements" and credit default swaps, The Levy Economics Institute of Bard College Policy Note 2009/9 [accessed on 24 November 2009] Available at http://www.levy.org/pubs/pn_09_09.pdf.
7. The view was given by the chair of the prominent law firm Sullivan & Cromwell, quoted in Noam Chomsky (2009). Crisis and Hope — Theirs and Ours Boston Review September/October [accessed on 16 September 2009] Available at http:// bostonreview.net/BR34.5/chomsky.php.

8. Noam Chomsky (2009).

9. Bill Bradley *et al.* (2009). *The Crisis and How to Deal with It, New York Review of Books*, 56(10), June 11.

10. Edward Carr (2009). Fixing Finance, *The Economist* 24 January 2009.

11. Robert M Solow (2009). *How to Understand the Disaster*, *The New York Review of Books*, 56(8), 14 May.

12. Robert Pollin (2009). Tools for a New Economy, *Boston Review*, January/February.

13. John Kay (1996). *The Business of Economics*, Oxford: Oxford University Press, p. 147.

14. Wang Xiaodong (2009). Disproportionate Share of Financial Industry Is a Sign of Decadence. In *Unhappy China: The Great Time, Grand Vision and Our Challenges*, Song Xiaojun, *et al.* (eds.), Nanjin: Jiangxu People's Publishing House (in Chinese).

15. Bill Bradley *et al.* (2009).

16. Michael Lim Mah Hui and Lim Chin (2010).

17. George Soros and Judy Woodruff (2008). The Financial Crisis: An Interview with George Soros, *New York Review of Books*, 15 May.

18. Jackson's Holes, *The Economist*, 29 August 2009.

19. Michael Heng Siam-Heng and Lim Tai Wei (2009). *Destructive Creati-vity of Wall Street and the East Asian Response*, Singapore: World Scientific.
    Pollin, R (2009).

20. Dummies for Finance, *The Economist*, 5 September 2009.

21. Paul Krugman (2008). *What to Do*, *New York Review of Books*, 18 December.

22. John Kay (2008). 'Too Big to Fail' Is Too Dumb to Keep, *Financial Times*, 28 October, p. 11.

23. George J Benston and George G Kaufman (1995). Is the Banking and Payments System Fragile? *Journal of Financial Services Research*, 9, 209–240.

24. George Soros and Judy Woodruff (2008). The Financial Crisis: An Interview with George Soros, *New York Review of Books*, 15 May.

25. It is like allowing a risk-loving driver to take part in Formula race but he is not allowed to take fellow passenger.

26. Lawrence Summers (1995). Ten Lessons to Learn, *The Economist*, 23 December 1995.

27. Stanley Fischer (1999). On the need for an international lender of last resort, talk delivered to the joint luncheon of the American Economic Association and The American Finance Association, New York, 3 January 1999, [accessed on 26 December 2008]. Available at www.imf.org/external/np/speeches/1999/010399.htm.

28. A system is robust if it can comfortably take small shocks, and it is resilient if it bounces back quickly after the small shocks. If the system fails to do so, then it is fragile.

29. Michael Lim Mah Hui and Lim Chin (2010). *Nowhere to Hide,* Singapore: ISEAS.

Chapter Nine

Globalization and All That

Globalization has been deeply affected by the financial crisis. As a result of the crisis, there has been a decline in capital movement, trade, and immigration. "Indeed, globalization itself is reversing," notes Roger Altman, a former US Deputy Treasury Secretary.[1] Though globalization is unlikely to be rolled back, it is likely to emerge in a different form after the crisis. At the same time, the crisis is speeding up the shift in the world political and economic orders that took shape after World War II. The clearest sign of this is the replacement of G8 by G20 as the forum of the world's economic powers. Just as the dominance of America is buttressed by its intellectual leadership, its financial and economic woes call into question its intellectual prowess in economic matters and the merits of its financial system.

In the midst of America's financial distress, it is easy to overlook the fact that its economic foundation is still strong. It is the home of Boeing, Apple, Intel, Microsoft, Google, and General Electric. It held $6.6 trillion of foreign assets at the end of 2008 while foreigners held $4.1 trillion of American government securities.[2] Uncle Sam remains the world's venture capitalist and his plight is not as bad as it seems.

Globalization

Global financial system and globalization are closely intertwined. On the one hand, global financial system is a product of globalization, deregulation, and advanced information technology. On the other hand, it epitomizes globalization and may be seen as the most advanced aspect of globalization. Supported by the system, money flows to where it is able to earn the highest profit, with the minimal interference from the state. Country with the best climate for doing business will earn the favors of international investment, be it equity fund or FDI. To advocates of globalization, such even playing field will spur economic development, reduce poverty, increase the flow of management know-how and technologies, and promote trade. Supporters of globalization have used such arguments to explain the star economic performance of East Asian countries. Globalization represents a historic opportunity for industrialization and modernization.

On the opposite side, critics have focused on sweat shops, export of pollution from rich countries, etc. Globalization is seen by left-wing intellectuals and social activists as a continuation of colonization and a new form of imperialism. The current recession will prompt social activists, scholars, and political leaders to engage themselves in reflecting on what globalization really means. Nations will recalibrate their policies in the light of the impact of the recession on their economies and societies.

The crisis highlights the fact that the global economic system is unstable. This point is best illustrated in the economic relationship between Asia and the USA. Asia needs the USA as its major export market. In addition, the later has to keep on borrowing money from the former to finance the imports as well as to cover the hole in the budget deficits. Though the trend has slowed down, it has not been drastically reversed. The situation is clearly unsustainable over long run. Meanwhile, the greenback is heading south, a reflection of the weakening US economy. Both sides are locked into an entangling embrace that neither side can afford to let go. It is a kind of dangerous and unstable economic relationship: "the mutually assured destruction that would ensue should either set of arms loosen".[3] It is therefore patently clear that global restructuring of the economy is needed. Thinkers, political leaders, economists, and other social scientists have much work cut out for them.

Realities of Globalization

In its purest form, globalization assumes that the whole world is one giant country. There is free flow of trade, capital, and people. Trade deficit is not an issue at all, for market mechanism will correct it. The state can take a back seat. Trade has no barrier and faces no tariff. People can move to where they can find work. But the international system today is still based on sovereign states and nationalism remains a potent ideology in most parts of the world. Conceptual purity of globalization is bound to run into many difficulties.

In spite of such reality, the idea of free capital flow has enjoyed a following among the leaders of most countries in the past several decades. They buy the neoliberal argument that financial liberalization and free capital flow will reap bountiful benefits for countries in an increasingly integrated world. Countries that exercise fiscal rectitude and prudent macroeconomic management will attract the favors of global capital, which will stimulate economic growth. To its critics, free capital flow is an excellent device for those in control of enormous financial resources to cream off the top layer of speculative profit whenever there is uncertainty in the international financial market. The Asian financial crisis has severely weakened the case for free capital flow. The current crisis has rendered another powerful blow to it. Those countries with financial liberalizations have suffered deeply while those with insulated financial systems have suffered the least economic upheaval. The reasons are not too hard to find. Before the advent of free capital movement, capital flows followed trade and investment, resulting in benefits for the parties concerned. Now, capital flows tend to produce distressing havocs to trade and long-term investment.[4] We are now facing the end of a particular form of globalization that was driven largely by a dramatic expansion of financial flows.[5]

In times of crisis, it is the state that shoulders the responsibility to look after its people. The international community plays only a helping role. Given this obvious fact, it is highly irresponsible on the part of neoliberals to advocate that the state should be rolled back. The neoliberal idea commanded a respectable following in the wake of the fall of the Berlin Wall. But on the watch of President Reagan, a world-class champion of neoliberalism, the state machinery did not really shrink. In fact, he increased the budget for the military. When Reagan, Mrs. Thatcher, and like-minded leaders implemented the policies of privatization and deregulation, business firms had more avenues to make money. But when AIG, Citigroup, and the likes run into disaster as a result of their own makings, the state is called upon to intervene and bail them out. This is nothing less than privatization of profits and socialization of losses. Seen in this light, can we see return of the state as a good thing? Has retreat of the state been partly responsible for their nation's decline? If the crisis could force a serious rethinking among the political elites, then the crisis should have come earlier.

In spite of the long move toward globalization in the past decades, sovereign states are still strategic players on the global scene. States, in contestation and negotiation with other strategic players such as transnational corporations, shape the trajectory of globalization. Its actual form and substance, working, and performance are shaped by culture, history, and institutional setups of the country in which it operates. The crisis gives some indications of the changes that are likely to happen to globalization as we go further down the road. We are seeing some change in trade patterns, reduced capital flows, creeping protectionism, and re-assessment of capital liberalization.[6]

Keynesian Stimuli and Globalization

The economic and social contexts of applying Keynesian stimuli have to be kept in mind. It is effective in a context of inadequate demand and over supply. More importantly, the nature of the demand is important. Consider two cases, A and B. In Case A, apples are rotting in the field while thousands are starving. In Case B, there is oversupply of cars when almost every one with a valid driving license has a car. Keynesian stimulus would work well in Case A but it will not work well in Case B. It does not make sense to encourage obese people to consume more beef just because there is oversupply of beef.

In fact, what the world urgently needs is to apply Keynesian stimuli at the global level. Translated into concrete actions, it means helping those who live in horrendous poverty to lead a more decent life — proper nourishment, clear water, basic healthcare, and education. Help them to break through the vicious cycle of poverty and join the global effort to achieve the millennium goal. John Keynes would be smiling in his resting place.

Countries emerging from abject poverty represent an attractive market for industries of the rich countries and a reduction in the sources of global instability. At the same time, it will soothe the conscience of the rich countries to help them.

> The inequities associated with globalization have long been evident to those concerned about global social justice. And, at least since the global financial crisis of 1997–1998, the instabilities of globalization have been a source of much anxiety. But the events of September 11 have added a new dimension to the globalization debate.... while the links between poverty and terrorism are complicated, few would deny that poverty, and especially high unemployment rates among young men, provide fertile ground on which terrorism can grow. Ensuring that globalization will be more helpful to the poor thus becomes not just a moral imperative but also something that should be viewed as a matter of self-interest.[7]

Within countries, globalization affects Keynesian stimuli too. In the context of fierce global competition, the nature and quality of fiscal spending to make up for lack of demand are important.[8] The worst form is to offer tax cuts to the rich who will hoard the money and there is no effect at all on the economy. The best form is to beef up social infrastructure to improve and upgrade the quality of the people, such as education, healthcare and social safety net. It is also the ideal preparation for the workforce to seize new opportunities in an economic upturn. It means investment in human capital for skill development, adaptability, and capacity to conceive and experiment with new ideas.[9]

China as the Last Flying Goose

Even before the outbreak of the financial crisis, sharp observers would argue that the world has had an overcapacity in manufacturing. This is very evident in automobile industry. This phenomenon is very well explained by Robert Brenner.[10] It holds serious implications for countries trying to modernize and industrialize along the trajectory pioneered by Japan and successfully followed by other East Asian countries. With the world market stuffed to overflowing with manufactured goods, what are big countries like India, Brazil, and Indonesia going to do? Small countries or small economies can be accommodated, especially if they are of strategic geopolitical importance. But big countries will find that they face immense difficulty in following Japan unless the followings happen: there is huge expansion of the middle class in China with big disposable income and Japan wakes up from its economic slumber and goes on a spending binge. These two scenarios are unlikely to happen in the near future.

Before the outbreak of the crisis, the question of manufacturing overcapacity could be pushed to the backstage. After all, the West seemed to exhibit an inexhaustible appetite and capacity in absorbing the manufactured goods. It was well known that the USA was living beyond its means. But as long as the going was good, far sighted and rational argument could find only a tiny audience. The crisis has brought the question to the agenda of the existing members of the flying geese and those who wish to join them.

Western consumers are working hard to repair their household balance sheets by cutting down consumption. Exports from East Asian countries to their traditional market in the West have plunged across the board, and they are unlikely to recover soon. The implication is that the current flying geese model is not sustainable, and China may well be the last member to have successfully joined the flight. What does it mean for other countries that want to modernize and industrialize? One response is to work for closer Asian integration in trade, investment, production, and consumption. But China, Japan, and South Korea are unlikely to provide the alternative export market for manufactured goods of their neighbors. There is a pressing need to look for new growth models.

Geopolitical Dimension

For America, the financial crisis broke out at a time when it was facing the twin deficits and was having a bad time in Afghanistan and Iraq. It certainly has affected its supreme position in the world. To assess its impact, some have turned to the past for guidance and insights. The Great Depression accelerated the decline of Britain and the rise of America. The world that emerges from this recession will be shaped largely by China and America, the one rising and the other declining as a global power.[11] Similar line of thinking has inspired the idea of G2, which argues that between them, America and China will decide the main issues facing the world. The idea of G2 is silly for the simple reason that it does not correspond with reality. It is a fact that America's geopolitical leadership is weakened; its intellectual leadership in economics and finance is challenged; the dollar as the world currency is being questioned. Though these are certainly not good news for Washington, it does not mean that America as Number One is over. The gap between the USA and China is still big on many fronts. Writing just before the Japanese general election, Yukio Hatoyama gives a succinct and realistic description of American global position[12]:

> I also feel that as a result of the failure of the Iraq war and the financial crisis, the era of U.S.-led globalism is coming to an end and that we are moving toward an era of multipolarity. But at present no one country is ready to replace the United States as the dominant country. Nor is there a currency ready to replace the dollar as the world's key currency. Although the influence of the U.S. is declining, it will remain the world's leading military and economic power for the next two to three decades.

Center of Global Financial System

It has been famously said that when the USA sneezes, the world catches a cold. Though America has descended a few steps from the commanding height, it still occupies the center in the global financial system. That position accrues America some critical advantages. Its standards for accounting and auditing are the *de facto* global standards. This gives tremendous power to US courts, regulators, and politicians over global investment throughout the world.[13]

Dollar as the World Currency

By virtue of the Bretton Woods agreement, the greenback became the world currency. Even after the demise of Bretton Woods, the dollar has continued to function as the world currency. Businesses prefer to use the currency in trade and investment. Countries prefer to use the dollar to keep their foreign reserves. This means that lots of money is left in the American financial system. Starting in the 1990s, East Asian countries have linked their currencies to the dollar, and have been holding their reserves in dollars. The arrangement allows the USA to continue to enjoy the political benefits of seigniorage. It gives America the right to acquire real resources by running the printing press. The resources are not just imported goods but the ability to deploy large military forces overseas without having to tax its own citizens to do so. "Every historian knows that a hegemonic currency is part of an imperial system of political relations. Americans acquiesced in the unbalanced economic relations initiated by East Asian governments in their undervaluation of their currencies because they ensured the persistence of unbalanced political relations."[14]

There is no credible alternative international currency willing and able to replace the dollar, at least not now. To be the world currency means that countries with trade surpluses would like to keep at least most of the money in that currency, let us say X. This means that issuer country of X must be willing to run deficits. Japan and the European Union are the only two large economies with credible world currency but they are not willing to run deficits. Though Japan's foreign reserves in the dollar is shrinking in value over the years, Japan is able to get American military protection. That may explain why Japan has been quick in buying the dollar to cover up American deficits. As this arrangement benefits both sides, the dollar as the world currency is unlikely to change unless there is a fundamental change in the world economic structure.

From Unipolar to Multipolar World

About 1970, at a time when the USA was clearly losing the Vietnam War, it was showing signs of decline. An unequivocal manifestation of this is the decision of the Nixon administration to suspend convertibility of dollar into gold in 1971. The White House also made demands on its allies to share the burden of maintenance costs of the US-centered world order. Various US administrations have tried to reverse the process of decline by various means.

> Some tried human rights diplomacy or some version of liberal measures. Others attempted more realist policies by expanding military capability or turning to high-tech military power such as 'Star Wars.' None were able to reverse the process, but everyone sought to find the most efficient way to manage the world with less power. What happened in recent years is that George W. Bush came along with the neocons who thought they were going to reverse this by policy of militarism and unilateralism. But instead of reversing the process and restoring US hegemony, they accelerated the process of decline.[15]

Now, the world economy is facing difficulties just as US hegemony is being questioned more seriously than before. The unipolar world that underlined the Bush foreign policy is definitely untenable. More and more countries are refusing to accept the unipolar world. Current crisis accentuates this trend. "This coincides with the movement away from a unipolar world, which the downturn has accelerated."[16] Unlike President Bush, President Obama has displayed a much better understanding of the real world outside the USA. His policies are more realistic, his words more conciliatory, and his manners more acceptable. The issue is no longer one of unipolarity versus multipolarity. The issue is how the world is going to manage multipolarity with a weakened superpower still shouldered with many international responsibilities while other powers have yet to design ways to work with the

Number One to resolve teething problems. G20 has so far proved to be no more than a global forum to make announcements whose outlines had been known beforehand. It will take some time for it to become an effective platform for decisive actions.

But with an economy showing anemic growth, Obama may be forced by domestic pressure to look inward and constrained by unemployment and fiscal pressures.[17] This immediately leads to two questions. First, with reduced resources and energies for global matters, would Washington deploy them mainly for its campaign against terrorism, leaving other matters which had attracted previous administrations to find their own solutions? Examples of such issues are the Israeli-Palestinian conflicts, climate change and North Korea.

Second, the US military machine is still the biggest and most powerful in the world. Its military budget is more than that of the next top 20 countries combined.[18] Would a weakened economic base be able to sustain such military expenditure? To what extent would its close allies be willing and able to share the burden? Would rogue states (real or so-called) be looking for chinks in US armor to create trouble? This is the kind of international order the Japanese leader Yukio Hatoyama was talking about.

Intellectual Influence

It has been noted earlier that at the end of the Cold War, the Anglo-Saxon model was making inroads in various corners of the world. "The role of the state was diminishing, and deregulation, privatization, and the openness of borders to capital and trade were rising. Much of central and eastern Europe adopted this model, as did swaths of East Asia and diverse nations from Ireland to Mexico."[19] The influence extends to matters beyond the realm of macroeconomic policies. Universities all over the world gradually move to the American system of management. Many parents who can afford the costs would prefer to send their children to universities in the USA. The Ivy League universities have become the natural venues for would-be global elites to nurture social networking.

The crisis has done much to disrupt this flow of events.

> Now, a page has been turned. The Anglo-Saxon financial system is seen as having failed. The global downturn, and all its human devastation, is being attributed to that failure. Throughout the world, including in the United States, this has turned the political tide in a new direction. The role of the state is expanding again, together with a reregulation of markets. This is evident in the United States and elsewhere.[20]

The economic recession leads naturally to questions concerning the intellectual edifice supporting the Anglo-American model of laissez faire capitalism. It touches on social policies, role of state, industrial policy, and even the nature of US democracy. For example, Alan Greenspan was appointed by President Reagan to head the Federal Reserve Board because he was the choice of Wall Street.[21] Does it make sense in the context of liberal democracy? Don't the opinions and interests of other communities, stakeholders, and, most important of all, the citizens carry more weight? All the more so when the financial system suffers a meltdown, it is the taxpayers who will foot the bills of bailouts and other rescue programs.

The World's Venture Capitalist

In the numerous and repeated reports on America's current account deficits, it is important to note that the USA held $6.6 trillion-worth of foreign shares and direct investments at the end of 2008. The amount was more than the $4.1 trillion government securities held by foreigners. This will help to correct the image that Uncle Sam is saddled heavily with debts and is in deep trouble. *The Economist* (3 October 2009) suggests that we can look at America as a venture capitalist.[22]

> America could offset the inflow of capital from foreign central banks with an outflow of capital of its own. It can borrow 'short' from emerging countries, satisfying their demand for safe, liquid securities, even as it invests 'long' in riskier but more rewarding assets overseas. ...It issues fixed-income liabilities and puts the money into shares and direct investments abroad. Its role as a venture capitalist is not merely a metaphor. The country accounts for the bulk of cross-border venture-capital deals. Between 2003 and 2007 the number of deals America carried out abroad exceeded the number that foreigners carried out in America by an average of 3,000 a year.[23]

There is an advantage for America if it invests heavily abroad. It would weaken the dollar, making it cheaper for foreigners to buy American goods, thereby improving America's trade balance. An export boom would do more than anything else to stir corporate America into action and get companies spending on R&D again.[24]

It would even be better if America lets other countries buy its technologies. China is cash rich, but it is badly in need of advanced technologies to help it clean up the environment and to embark on the next level of economic development based on high-tech. The solution is pretty straightforward if Washington upholds the spirit of globalization. Would China not use some of its vast foreign reserves to buy the needed technology from the West? With a depressed market, China is in a good position to strike a good bargain. For China, this is far better than to see its dollar shrink in real value with each passing day. For the West, China represents one of the few markets that have the money to buy their high-tech. As long as it does not involve military technology, there is no valid political argument to block high-tech sale.

Another way to reduce the current account imbalance is for the West to welcome sovereign wealth funds to buy their assets. The Middle East oil states, Singapore, and China have mountains of cash but they have faced politically motivated opposition when they try to invest in the West. In spite of repeated assurances by the SWFs, Western governments still believe that SWFs function like the financial fifth columns of their governments.

Endnotes

1. Roger C Altman (2009). Globalization in Retreat. *Foreign Affairs*, 88(4), 2–7.

2. Simon Cox (2009). Industrial Design, *The Economist*, 3 October.

3. R Taggart Murphy (2009). In the Eye of the Storm: Updating the Economics of Global Turbulence, an Introduction to Robert Brenner's Update, *The Asia-Pacific Journal*, 49-1-09 December 7.

4. Richard C Koo (2009). *The Holy Grail of Macroeconomics*, revised and updated edition, Singapore: John Wiley.

   Michael Lim Mah Hui and Lim Chin (2010). Nowhere to Hide, Singapore: ISEAS.

5. Horold James (2008). The End of a Gilded Age, 1 December. [accessed on 17 November 2009]. Available at http://www.project-syndicate.org/commentary/james21.

6. Roger C Altman (2009).

7. Joseph E Stiglitz (2002). A Fair Deal for the World, *New York Review of Books*, 49(9).

8. Richard C Koo (2009).

9. Mihir Rakshit (2002). *The East Asian Currency Crisis*, New Delhi: Oxford University Press.

10. Robert Brenner (2003). *The Boom and the Bubble: The US in the World Economy*, London.

    Robert Brenner (2006). *The Economics of Global Turbulence*, London: Verso.

11. Harold James (2009). *The Creation and Destruction of Value: The Globalisation Cycle*, Cambridge, MA: Harvard University Press.

12. Yukio Hatoyama (2009). A New Path for Japan, *The New York Times* [accessed on 10th September 2009]. Available at http://www.nytimes.com/2009/08/27/opinion/27iht-edhatoyama.html.

13. Kenneth Rogoff (2009). Brave New Financial World, Project Syndicate [accessed on 10 November 2009]. Available at

http://www.koreatimes.co.kr/www/news/opinon/2009/03/137_42153.html.

14. Robert Skidelsky (2009). The World Financial Crisis and the American Mission, *The New York Review of Books*, 56(12).

15. Immanuel Wallerstein and Jae Jung Suh (2009). Capitalism's Demise? *The Asia–Pacific Journal*, 8 January.

16. Roger C Altman (2009).

17. Roger C Altman (2009).

18. World Global Spending. [accessed on 18 January 2010] Available at http://www.globalissues.org/article/75/world-military-spending#USMilitarySpending.

19. Roger C Altman (2009).

20. Altman, RC (2009).

21. Alan Greenspan (2007). *The Age of Turbulence*, New York: The Penguin Press.

22. Pierre-Olivier Gourinchas of the University of California, Berkeley, and Hélène Rey of the London Business School have described America as the world's "venture capitalist". Please see Simon Cox (2009). Industrial Design, *The Economist*, 3 October.

23. Simon Cox (2009).

24. *Ibid*.

Chapter Ten

Don't Waste the Crisis

Disaster is that on which good fortune depends.
Good fortune is that in which disaster's concealed.
Who knows where it will end?

Tao-Te Ching by Laozi
(translated by Robert G. Henricks)[1]

The current recession has been long and painful, and recovery is likely to be weak and slow. The structural issues to speed up recovery are not easy to overcome. While this presents a grave challenge, it also provides an occasion for people to rethink basic issues and address long-term problems. The present crisis makes it important to face the neglected long-term issues such as conservation of the environment and national health care, as well as the need for public transport.[2] If long-term issues are handled well, the recession may herald a long wave of technological innovations and robust economic growth. This has happened in the past and the cycle is known as Kondratieff Cycle. At the same time, the crisis prompts economists to re-examine their pet theories. Economics may emerge as a more empirically grounded, socially relevant, and intellectually respectable discipline.

243

A Slow and Weak Recovery

At the height of the current crisis in late 2008, there was fear of the crisis slipping into a depression. Since then, things did brighten up substantially, and the general consensus is that the worst is over. There were talks of green shoots and real recovery. However, there are reasons to believe that the recovery will be slow and weak. The financial sector has certainly staged a recovery strong enough for financial firms on life support system to want to leave the Troubled Asset Relief Program. Even assuming that their recovery is based on decent profits, the same cannot be said of the broad spectrum of US business firms. Without a solid performance of the real economy, it is difficult to see how long-term recovery of the financial sector can be sustained.

Martin Feldstein of Harvard University cautions us not to think that the economy can recover as before. He says:

> Previous recessions were often characterized by excess inventory accumulation and overinvestment in business equipment. The economy could bounce back as those excesses were absorbed over time, making room for new investment. Those recoveries were also helped by interest rate reductions by the central bank. This time, however, the fall in share prices and in home values has destroyed more than $12 trillion of household wealth in the United States, an amount equal to more than 75 percent of GDP. Previous reactions to declines in household wealth indicate that such a fall will cut consumer spending by about $500 billion every year until wealth is restored.[3]

The loss of such wealth effect, combined with bleak economic outlook and high unemployment, depresses consumption. As a result, economic growth driven by consumption will be slow.

Moreover, debt-financed spending has left households with a balance sheet problem. "Whereas most recessions follow a sequence of rising inflationary pressures, monetary tightening to counter them, and a slowdown in response to higher interest rates, this one is a balance-sheet-driven recession. It is rooted in the financial damage to households and banks from the housing- and credit-market collapse."[4] Balance-sheet recession is the worst form of recessions.[5] As testified by the Japanese experience, balance-sheet recession is deep and painful, and the recovery process is slow and long.

Households will strive to repair their balance sheets by diverting an increasing part of their incomes to replenish depleted assets, not only in 401Ks, but in the value of their homes as well.[6] Consumption spending is set to decline until the whole repair exercise is largely completed. According to *The Economist* (3 October 2009), net worth of households amounts to 487 percent of their disposable income, down from a historical average of about 500 percent. To restore their wealth to this average, households would have to clear about $1.4 trillion of debt. At their present rate of saving, the process will not be finished until 2012.[7] According to another estimate, even with a higher household saving rate, it would take more than a decade of relatively high saving rates to restore what was lost.[8]

When households are holding back on spending, business firms will be hesitant in production and investment.

The shortfall in demand can guide the economy into a downward spiral. The danger has been averted so far by keeping interest rates at near zero and aggressive fiscal prime pumping. But fiscal stimuli in the USA can continue only for a limited period because of its galloping budget deficits.

A drop of demand in the US means that the world can no longer depend on Uncle Sam's spending as a way out as in the past. The fall of demand in the USA and Europe is truly bad news for those countries that have in the past depended on them as export markets to get out of economic downturn. This time round, the world depends on countries with large foreign currency reserves to make up for the global demand shortfall.

> Quite simply, the rest of the world must spend more while the US should spend less and save more and production in the US must go up, without boosting domestic consumption. Such burden sharing would in the medium and probably long-term result in a visibly lower US share of global Gross Domestic Product and a larger Chinese one.[9]

Indeed, Beijing's policy response to the global economic malaise is to boost domestic demand and consumption. It unveiled a huge stimulus package in November 2008.[10] The targets of government spending are (a) transport infrastructure (45 percent), (b) reconstruction in areas hit by recent earthquakes (25 percent), (c) rural infrastructure (9 percent), (d) environmental improvement (9 percent), (e) public housing (7 percent), (f) R&D (4 percent), and (g) healthcare and education (1 percent). The total cost for the first two years of these projects is about Rmb4 trillion ($586 billion).

Here a few words about consumption may be in order. Consumption often invokes the image of consumerism, with money spent on eating and drinking, clothes and jewelries, and cars and holidays. But consumption is necessary for us to survive, grow, and develop our potentials. Giving milk to babies is consumption, and it is perhaps the best example of *productive consumption*. Just like investment, consumption can be economically productive and socially useful, or economically wasteful and socially useless. In fact, in many cases, the boundary between consumption and investment is pretty fuzzy.[11]

Four areas where the Chinese government needs to put in more money are healthcare, education, affordable housing, and pension system. In short, the Beijing government would do well to weave a social welfare and safety net that provides real substance to its socialism with Chinese characteristics. China has the financial means to implement a modest scheme of social welfare, given its growing economy and fiscal surpluses over the past years. Moreover it has the moral obligation to do so because its breakneck GDP growth in the past two decades has not adequately trickled down to the working masses. For example, employment has grown by just 1 percent per annum in recent years. The share of wages and other household income in GDP has fallen from 72 percent in 1992 to 55 percent in 2007.[12]

In an interesting way, the idea of social welfare and safety net is contained in the Chinese term for economy – 经济 (*jinji*). The Chinese took it from the Japanese translation 经济 (*keizai*), which is derived from the twin ideas of 经国 (*jinguo*) and 济民 (*jimin*) in ancient Chinese text. 经国 means running the country or governing the state while 济民 means assisting the people, especially when they are in need. The concept of *jinji* in Chinese or *keizai* in Japanese contains the idea of social welfare as part of the economic order, just as it is being practiced in Western Europe. Perhaps the dichotomy between the Western and Eastern civilizations is exaggerated. Perhaps, the USA is more an exception rather than the norm in the rich Western economies.

Kondratieff Cycle in the Making?

The current crisis evokes a renewed interest in the Great Depression of the 1930s. Harking further back, there was the Long Depression of 1873–1896, which possessed remarkable similarities with the current recession. Seemingly new crises and their policy debates are often variants of past crises and debates, especially once a serious crisis in a given country is seen to have broader international context.[13]

The Long Depression was preceded by a period of strong economic growth in Western Europe and North America.[14] The end of the American Civil War (1861–1865) saw the beginning of a boom in railway construction. Between 1866 and 1873, 56,000 kilometers of new track was laid across the country. The railway network enjoyed tremendous confidence of banks and investment community. To them, it had all the beautiful qualities of a good investment — low risk, good return, and growth. The railway companies issued bonds that were pooled together just like securitization now and sold to investors. Cheap money resulted in over-building of docks, factories, and all kinds of construction projects. Like the subprime episode, the true picture slowly emerged. In early 1870s, the forecasts turned out to be too rosy. The trigger was the tight monetary policy that the US adopted in order to get back to the gold standard after the Civil War. In September 1873, the interest rates rose sharply. The railway companies could not service the loans. Investors dumped the bonds and the major bank in the game, Jay Cook & Company, went under.

A similar wave of over confident speculation hit Europe too. In Germany, euphoria over military victory against France in 1871, together with war reparation money from France, set off a wave of stock market speculation in railways, factories, docks, and steamships. On top of this, there was a bubble in real estate. Around 1870, Berlin, Vienna, and Paris were the scenes of construction boom. Land prices rose and the expectation was that property prices would continue to rise. Based on such belief, developers could have access to easy credit, adding fuel to the frenzy.

At the same time, European agriculture was facing competition from the US where the sector was increasingly modernized. Cheap imports pushed European agriculture into a corner. From May 1873, Austrian banks began to go bust because their clients in the agricultural sector could no longer service their loans. The trouble spread to other sectors and in the same month the Vienna Stock Exchange crashed. Vienna was soon followed by Berlin and then Paris.

Governments in Europe and America responded to the crisis by protectionism and exporting their trouble to their colonies. The colonies thus served as the safety valve for the crisis. It also led to a renewed scramble for new colonies and rivalries among the colonial powers. This was the background behind Cecil Rhodes' famous remark that imperialism was a "bread-and-butter" question. The crisis became a worldwide economic crisis, sucking remote corners of the world into the man-made disaster.

However, with the end of the Long Depression, Europe, the USA, and Japan experienced a period of economic growth and development that continued until the outbreak of World War I. The recession and subsequent robust economic growth are two stages of what is often known as a Kondratieff cycle. It refers to a long business cycle, with recession, but also wave of technological innovations that generally accompanies major economic downturns.

The post-Long Depression period was a *belle époque* of optimism and socioeconomic transformation.[15] Telephones, bicycles, motorcycles, cars, airplanes, and synthetic chemistry made their appearance. Towns were bright with lights at night. Cars slowly displaced horse carriages on the roads. Mobility of population inside and outside national borders increased tremendously. The same applied to capital that moved from financial capitals such as London, Berlin, and Paris to Moscow, New York, and other corners. Trade unions sprang up to defend the rights of workers and they were able to wrestle concessions from their bosses. Their living and working conditions improved, which led to better health and higher work productivity.

Sociopolitical institutions demonstrated ability and flexibility in responding to emergent social changes. Economic growth was self-sustaining. It was a period of urbanization and change in consumption pattern. As a way to coordinate international trade and finance, the Gold Standard was adopted, based on a monetary system that had evolved over the preceding centuries. Under this arrangement, national currencies were fully convertible and the exchange rates fluctuated within a very small band. This discouraged short-term capital movements and promoted trade and long-term foreign investments. Technological innovation, financial stability, and social peace underpinned an impressive virtuous cycle of capitalist growth that was surpassed in intensity, duration, and geographical scope by the period 1950–1973. Real average wages increased and technical progress gradually reduced the length of working hours.

The historical experiences of the Long Depression offer some insights for the current recession. The first insight is outlined in Chapters 6 and 8 on reforming the financial system. The financial sector must be made to serve the real economy and not the other way round. If Wall Street continues to hold the rest of the economy captive, then the road to recovery will be much longer and tortuous. The second insight is the need for productivity and technological innovation. The third is the importance of looking after the welfare of workers and instituting progressive social reforms.

Productivity and Technological Innovation

Economic recession subjects firms and industries to intense heat in the crucible of competition. It is natural for governments to come under pressure to save and support sunset and dying industries. But this is wrong, for it is an exercise in investing in the past, not in the future. Those industries too weak to survive in the new environment should be left to disappear but the affected workers must be assisted and retrained to work in the more promising industries. In the present context, examples of such industries are those that promote sustainable growth, green technologies, and biomedical sector.

Investing in the future means pumping money into socially useful research and supporting private sectors to build more plants and equipment to capture the results of such research. It also means improving social infrastructure, especially improving the quality of basic and pre-university education. It is an old story that has proved to work well in success stories of economic growth. It provides the knowledge base and human resources for productivity and technological innovations.

On the question of innovation, a few words on the information economy may be in order. At the height of the dot-com euphoria, powerful voices were claiming that the information economy was different. We were told that we had entered the era of new economy with a different set of logics. The banking and financial industry is seen as a prototypical industry in the information economy. It deals with data and information, and uses computer as its work horse. Here brains are more valued than muscles. Such general observations do not raise the crucial question: in what way does it add value to the customers. Even more important, in what way does it add value to society? In a lecture in 1984, Nobel economics laureate James Tobin says something very prescient[16]:

> I [suspect] we are throwing more and more of our resources, including the cream of our youth, into financial activities remote from the production of goods and services, into activities that generate high private rewards disproportionate to their social productivity. I suspect that the immense power of the computer is being harnessed to this 'paper economy,' not to do the same transactions more economically but to balloon the quantity and variety of financial exchanges ... I fear that, as Keynes saw even in his day, the advantages of the liquidity and negotiability of financial instruments come at the cost of facilitating nth-degree speculation which is short-sighted and inefficient.

Social Welfare

Though the crisis has hit the Western world equally hard, the impact on the people in those European countries with social welfare schemes is much more benign than that in the USA. It is heartening to note therefore that Paul Krugman, for example, has been championing for a strong safety net to be implemented in the USA.[17] To him, it is part of a civilized social order. Society is a huge social unit made up of many individuals who both contribute to it and make demands on it. Without such bondage and mutual obligations, a society falls apart. In other words, a society that refuses to pay a small cost to preserve equitable and fair treatment of the sick, the old, the unemployed, the disadvantaged and the victims of natural disaster is not much of a society.[18]

It is a well-known social and political fact that economic destitution and social injustice breed social unrest, which can easily degenerate into social instability. Yet social peace is so much needed to promote virtuous cycle of economic growth, as testified by the post-Long Depression recovery. When economists argue for strong safety net, they have history on their side, interests of the people and nation in their hearts, and economic recovery in their minds. That means rolling back the influence of neoliberalism at the level of policy making. "One of the gravest dangers to economic recovery lies precisely in the political classes' inflexible commitment to the neo-liberal economic order."[19]

Economics as a Social Science

As Keynes points out, economics ideas do shape policy.[20] The neo-liberal economic policy followed by the US administration over the past few decades has been deeply shaped by neo-liberal thinking. In a certain sense, the crisis is also intellectual — a systematic failure of thinking on the part of the majority of mainstream economists.[21] It is a good thing that the crisis has stirred up a heated debate among economists, other social scientists, and social philosophers. In fact, economics as an academic discipline may be invigorated and may prove to be one of the few beneficiaries of the crisis. It has been pointed out by John Galbraith that "the study of economics responds well to visible misfortune and despair; success, self-approval and satisfaction provide no similar inspiration."[22]

One fruitful outcome is a sustained critique of the efficient market theory so favored by the neo-liberals. They believe that unbridled market is the best and most efficient mechanism for delivering goods and services. When things go wrong, it is due to state intervention, such as bailouts and industrial policies. Market fundamentalism certainly suffers a serious dent because of the financial crisis, especially when their arch practitioners — Wall Street bankers — pleaded for state bailouts at the height of the crisis. The crisis has produced a rich body of literature which critically examines the assumptions, actual workings, and consequences of the efficient market theory.[23]

Besides putting market fundamentalism under the microscope, the current recession offers a good occasion to look at the followings:

1. Mainstream economic research has strayed away from the essence of social science, which pays due attention to social reality. Young researchers of economics can be forgiven if they think that most economics research published in top journals today has become a subset of applied mathematics. It is full of mathematical models and reads like an academic exercise in using advanced mathematics. Outside the circle of the converted, it certainly has a rarefied feel and touch. Apparently, social reality is less important than logical elegance and mathematical beauty. As if anticipating this phenomenon, the American economist Thorstein Veblen makes a distinction between two types of knowledge — esoteric knowledge and exoteric knowledge.[24] The first is of high prestige but

low practical value and the second is of low prestige but of high practical value. Like other great economists, the British economist Alfred Marshall favored realism and explanatory power of the theory, not logical coherence and formal elegance.

2. Pretty similar to the love for mathematical models, research economists show a penchant for deriving formulae that solve an equation to the nth decimal point. They can certainly profit from an advice of Aristotle in his *The Nicomachean Ethics*[25]:

> It is a mark of a trained mind never to accept more precision in the treatment of any subject than the nature of that subject permits.…

A similar piece of advice is given by John Keynes who prefers "to see the truth obscurely and imperfectly rather than to maintain error, reached indeed with clearness and consistency and by easy logic, but on hypothesis inappropriate to the facts."[26]

3. Economists need to rethink the way we measure economic activities. It has been known for a long time that environmental impacts are not factored in the pricing of natural resource products. "We have an economic counting scheme that celebrates all resource-using activity as growth while remaining suspicious of the full use of human resources, counting 'full employment' as a potential threat to profitability and inflation."[27]

4. Economic activities occur in social, cultural, political, and historical contexts. It is a sad story that

economics study nowadays is very narrowly focused, often devoid of its rich societal context and is non-historical. It runs the risk of going down the slippery slope to social irrelevance. It is submitted that economists need to return to the broad intellectual and empirical tradition of the great economists. The works of the great economists are a study of economic issues richly informed by sociology, history, and philosophy and this feature is very evident in the writings of Adam Smith, Karl Marx, Joseph Schumpeter, and John Keynes.

5. There is a central issue of creating value for the users of the product and society. Long-term growth is based on productivity improvement. "In the long run growth depends on replacing obsolete methods of production with better ones, and supplanting old industries with new ones."[28] We need to go back to basics and eschew all kinds of gimmicks. Assets inflation is an easy way to increase GDP. But it is unreliable and may well lead to long-term social and economic problems. By any stretch of imagination, it cannot build the competitive capacity of a country in a globalized economy.

6. Banking may stimulate, inhibit, or accommodate economic growth. Under what conditions and context is finance likely to play a beneficial or disruptive role in economic activities? The current crisis is a good example of how finance has played a destructive role. It has also grown too big. We need to know the appropriate size of the financial sector for a given economy.

Financial Crisis as Symptom of Deeper Problems

Financial system is part of the bigger economic system. As noted in Chapter 1, the abnormal growth of the financial system in the past decades is an easy-way-out response of the USA (and to a less extent Western Europe) to the emergence of East Asia as adroit manufacturing powers. Such failure to face up to the challenge in a positive way is also reflected in a range of other policies, including foreign policies, as argued by Kishore Mahbubani in his recent book.[29]

The direction of resources to financial sector is a failure of the old industrial powers to make a concerted effort at societal level to aim at a quantum leap in innovation across a broad spectrum of technologies. An American friend e-mailed me the following:

> It is sad to note that the USA has been sliding down the slope since its misadventure in Vietnam. This is reflected in the declining value of the greenback. More crucially, we have suffered a relentless decline of competitive edge in manufacturing, especially when compared with Japan. On the watch of Greenspan and his team, the USA has reinvented itself as a casino state at a time when it should be doing its best to make good use of the peace dividends in the post Cold War period and to cope with the challenges of a post 9/11 situation. It has channeled many scientific and mathematical talents to unproductive and (as it has turned out) destructive creativities. We foolishly and blindly soldered our economy, academy, and culture to a financial

machine that goes against the very core spirits of our founding fathers. The money class could have followed the footsteps of Silicon Valley entrepreneurs and become key players in nurturing new and socially useful industries. Instead they have opted to become rentiers. In the process Wall Street has degenerated to become cancer of US economy.

Because what happens now is a concentrated expression of an ongoing trend from the past, the essence of the underlying problems remains the same. Political leaders are thus looking at the same set of painful choices as their predecessors did before but in more difficult economic conditions. However, it presents them with a golden historic opportunity to open a discussion of how to move in the direction of a better world. A critical point on the agenda should be: vast reduction of military budgets to deal with only national defense and to channel the resources thus freed up to clean up the environment and help poor countries to develop. It is an age-old story of turning swords into ploughs. Sadly, such optimistic thinking is not supported by the outcome of the climate-change summit in Copenhagen.

If the financial crisis can be seen as a symptom of some deep societal malaises, then it provides an occasion to concentrate the minds of the intellectuals and political leadership to rethink their policies and to galvanize their nations to reform their systems. It is thus an opportunity to discard flawed policies and dysfunctional practices, to increase societal resources and to embark on the lofty task of society building. This remark certainly applies to the USA, which faces a host of social problems, either directly or indirectly related to its economy. To different degrees, the same can be said of other countries as well.

At the same time, the financial crisis reveals much that has gone wrong in the business world in the last few decades — short-term thinking, manipulation of figures, and image management at the cost of the basics. The financial sector has become an arena for accounting shenanigans and corporate skullduggery. The crisis is also a symptom of deeper cultural change. Crisis of this nature has the potential to function as a cleansing exercise — harmful ideas and values are likely to perish. Old ideas that are good are likely to survive and gain more influence while fresh ideas can germinate and grow. Already we have seen debates that re-examine values and ideas underpinning policy formulation and execution. This represents another serious challenge facing the global community. If the world could rise to the challenge, history would view the crisis as a blessing in disguise and thus a good crisis. Such thinking is certainly not wishful thinking, for history has shown time and again that crisis could be transformed into an opportunity for reform and rejuvenation.

As to whether the crisis has really functioned as a wakeup call and a shock to cause change, all the signs are that the current crisis is not big enough. Perhaps the world is waiting for a bigger one.

Endnotes

1. Laozi (1992). *Tao-Te Ching* (translated by Robert, G. Henricks), New York: Random House, Chapter 58.

A similar translation is done by John C. H. Wu in Lao Tzu (1989). *Tao Teh Ching*. Boston: Shambhala:

> "Bad fortune is what good fortune leans on,
> Good fortune is what bad fortune hides in,
> Who knows the ultimate end of this process?"

2. Amartya Sen (2009). Capitalism Beyond the Crisis, *New York Review of Books*, 26 March.
3. Martin Feldstein (2008). The Black Hole in America's GDP, *Project Syndicate*, 1 December [accessed 18 November 2009]. Available at http://www.project-syndicate.org/commentary/feldstein7.
4. Roger C Altman (2009). Globalization in Retreat, *Foreign Affairs*, 88(4), 2–7.
5. Richard C Koo (2009). *The Holy Grail of Macroeconomics*, revised and updated edition, Singapore: John Wiley.
6. Alan Greenspan (2008). Testimony to Committee of Government Oversight and Reform, 23 October [accessed on 9 December 2008]. Available at http://oversight.house. gov/index.php?option=com_content&task=view&id= 3470&Itemid=2.
7. Simon Cox (2009). From Ozzie to Ricky, *The Economist*, 3 October.
8. Martin Feldstein (2008). The Black Hole in America's GDP, *Project Syndicate*, 1 December [accessed 18 November 2009]. Avaiblable at http://www.project-syndicate.org/commentary/feldstein7.
9. Jurgen Møller (2009). *Political Economy in a Globalized World*, Singapore: World Scientific, p. 112.
10. Yang Mu and Lim Tin Seng (2009). How Severe Is China's Economic Downturn? *East Asian Institute Background Brief*, No. 437, National University of Singapore.

11. Peter Drucker (1990). *The New Realities*, London: Mandarin.

12. Simon Cox (2009). The Hamster-Wheel, *The Economist*, 3 October.

13. Harold James (2009). *The Creation and Destruction of Value: The Globalisation Cycle*, Cambridge, MA: Harvard University Press.

14. Panic of 1873 [accessed 20 November 2009]. Available at http://en.wikipedia.org/wiki/Panic_of_1873.

    Long Depression, From Wikipedia [accessed 20 November 2009]. Available at http://en.wikipedia.org/wiki/Long_Depression.

    The Long Depression: 1873–1896 [accessed 20 November 2009]. Available at http://www.bankcrash.nl/english/historythelongdepression.php.

    Raymond F Betts, *Europe in Retrospect* [accessed 20 November 2009]. Available at http://www.britannia.com/history/euro/2/2_1.html.

15. Ernesto Screpanti and Stefano Zamagni (1995). *An Outline of the History of Economic Thought*. Oxford: Clarendon Press.

16. Edward Carr (2009). Fixing Finance, *The Economist*, 24 January 2009.

17. Bill Bradley *et al.* (2009). The Crisis and How to Deal with It, *New York Review of Books*, 56(10), 11 June.

18. Robert Solow (2008). Trapped in the New "You're on Your Own" World, *The New York Review of Books*, 55(18), 20 November.

19. Financial and monetary issues as the crisis unfolds; Public Policy Brief, Highlights No. 103A, 2009; The Levy Economics Institute of Bard College.

20. Keynes concluded his masterwork, *The General Theory of Employment, Interest and Money*, with a famous note on the importance of economic ideas: "Soon or late, it is ideas, not vested interests, which are dangerous for good or evil."

21. Benjamin Friedman (2009). The Failure of the Economy & the Economists, *New York Review of Books*, 28 May 2009.

22. John K Galbraith (1987). *A History of Economics*, London: Penguin Books.

23. See for example, Michael Lim Mah Hui and Lim Chin (2010). *Nowhere to Hide*, Singapore: ISEAS, and various issues of *The New York Review of Books*, columns of Paul Krugman, papers posted on the website of The Levy Economics Institute of Bard College, and commentaries on website of Project Syndicate.

24. John K Galbraith (1987), p. 299.

25. Quoted in Mihir Rakshit (2002). The East Asian Currency Crisis, New Delhi: Oxford University Press.

26. John M Keynes (1936). *The General Theory of Employment, Interest and Money*, New York: Prometheus Books, p. 371.

27. Financial and monetary issues as the crisis unfolds; Public Policy Brief, Highlights No. 103A, 2009; The Levy Economics Institute of Bard College.

28. Simon Cox (2009). Market Fatigue, *The Economist*, 3 October.

29. Kishore Mahbubani (2008). *The New Asian Hemisphere: The Irresistible Shift of Global Power to the East*, New York: Global Affairs.

Index

Accounting shenanigan
    148, 260
added value   106
AIG   159, 166, 216, 229
Anglo-American   10,
    13, 26–28, 115, 140, 238
Apple   110, 225
Argentine   58
Aristotle   12, 192, 256
ASEAN   28, 29, 60, 68
Asian Monetary Fund   67,
    220
Asian Tigers   61, 65
Austria   212

Bair, Sheila   143
balance sheet recession
    79, 100, 158, 245
Baltic states   135
Beijing   67, 247
Berlin   5, 10, 17, 23, 25,
    26, 28, 30, 32, 35,
    51, 52, 66, 228, 249,
    250

Berlin Wall   5, 10, 17, 23,
    25, 26, 28, 30, 32, 35,
    51, 52, 66, 228
Blinder, Alan   63, 183
Boesky, Ivan   35
Brazil   9, 15, 52, 231
Brenner, Robert   3, 231
Bretton Woods   13, 219, 234
Britain   1, 42, 44, 45, 107,
    109, 126, 127, 233
Brown, Gordon   45, 179
Buffett, Warren   187
Buiter, Willem   209

California   82
Carter   24, 162
Casino   143, 161, 169, 221,
    222, 258
central bank   34, 81, 126,
    203, 205, 211, 212, 217,
    221, 239, 244
China   15, 16, 30, 31, 67,
    99, 100, 107, 111, 130,
    190, 231–233, 240, 247

Citigroup   11, 144, 145,
      151, 185, 229
City of London   27, 34, 45,
      140, 150, 179
Clinton   30, 35, 132, 144,
      159
Cold War   25, 26, 28, 29,
      46, 51, 59, 66, 67, 99,
      237, 258
collateralized debt obligation
      (CDO)   145, 165
Consumer Financial
      Protection Agency   206
Consumption   7, 18, 30, 51,
      69, 82, 85, 89, 92, 93,
      106, 142, 158, 213, 232,
      245, 246, 247, 251
creative destruction   29,
      102
credit   6, 7, 9, 11, 40, 55,
      56, 60, 63, 64, 67, 72,
      78, 87, 88, 97, 100, 104,
      109, 126, 130, 131, 133,
      142, 143, 148, 154,
      156–160, 165, 180, 184,
      205, 206, 212–216, 220,
      222, 245, 249
credit default swaps (CDS)
      11, 131, 143, 154, 159,
      165
credit expansion   56
currency crisis   52, 57, 68

Current account   58, 61, 62,
      68, 70, 91, 106, 142,
      220, 239, 240
custodian system   214
customer   38, 39, 154, 199,
      215, 216, 252

Davos   12, 188
Debt   55, 56, 61, 67, 82, 83,
      86, 100, 109, 112, 125,
      129, 131, 142, 144, 145,
      149, 158, 159, 165, 166,
      185, 205, 239, 245
Democratic Party of Japan
      46, 114
Deng Xiaoping   31, 107
deregulation   2, 9, 10, 24,
      30, 32, 34, 44, 66, 106,
      134, 139, 154, 157, 158,
      167, 168, 179, 208, 226,
      228, 237
derivatives   6, 11, 32, 139,
      158, 159, 168, 203, 207,
      208, 210, 212, 216
Detroit   177, 178
dot-com boom   10
Dow Jones Industrial
      Average   126
Drucker, Peter   38, 146

East Asia   4, 5, 8, 9, 24, 28,
      51–53, 59–62, 65, 66,

68, 77, 99, 226, 231,
232, 234, 235, 238, 258
Erste Bank   212
Euro   9, 24–26, 34, 44, 45,
57, 60, 69, 78, 80, 100,
116, 127, 134–136, 186,
211, 235, 238, 246,
248–250, 253, 258

Faustian deal   45
Feldstein, Martin   162,
244
Ferguson, Niall   162
financial architecture   219
financial crisis   1, 2, 7,
9–11, 14, 17, 18, 27, 28,
56, 59, 64, 66, 87, 89,
91, 104, 111, 125, 126,
134, 141–143, 179, 183,
188, 193, 203, 204, 208,
214, 220, 225, 228,
230–233, 255, 258, 259,
260
financial engineering   55,
149, 164, 216
financial reform   188
Fiscal deficits   7, 61, 142
fiscal stimulus   82, 165
Flying Geese   78, 104, 111,
232
Ford   7, 11, 24, 93, 95, 178,
227, 238, 247

Four Asian Tigers   61
Four Little Dragons   61
Friedman, Milton   23, 30,
32

G20   131, 225, 237
Galbraith, John   254
Geithner, Timothy   182,
205
General Motors   110
Gini coefficient   42
Global Financial Stability
Report 127, 130, 133
Globalization   10, 16, 36,
46, 78, 105, 106, 111,
125, 132, 134, 135, 167,
190, 225–231, 240
Goldman Sachs   8, 109,
144, 185
Google   20, 37, 110, 225
Great Depression   1, 23,
125, 162, 204, 208, 212,
233, 248
Greed   2, 3, 35, 39, 117,
132, 141, 144, 150, 153,
157, 161, 178–181
Greenspan, Alan   11, 26, 34,
64, 126, 141, 144, 155,
156, 159, 161, 188, 189,
238

Haier   100

Hatoyama, Yukio   46, 115, 116, 233, 237

Healthcare   15, 32, 41, 42, 94, 111, 188, 230, 231, 246, 247

Hedge funds   32, 54, 60, 67, 131, 140, 159, 165, 186, 217

Ho Kwon Ping   181, 189

Hong Kong   52, 60, 61, 67

Hoover, Herbert   125

Huawei   100

Hubris   9, 10

IMF   18, 58, 59, 63–65, 67, 69, 70, 126, 127, 130, 131, 133, 135, 163, 184, 188, 209, 220, 221

income disparities   41, 190

India   15, 16, 25, 111, 231

Indonesia   15, 52, 53, 55, 61, 63, 67, 231

Internet   4, 27, 29, 215

Investment funds   32, 54, 82, 145

IT, information technology   29, 134, 167, 226

Japan   3, 24, 59, 77, 127, 141, 186, 211, 231, 250

Jinji   247, 248

Johnson, Simon   209

Kay, John   36, 45, 210

Keizai   94, 247, 248

Keynes, John M   51

Keynesian   5, 8, 18, 83, 229–231

Koizumi   85, 115

Kondratieff cycle   243, 248, 250

Koo, Richard   88, 100

Krugman, Paul   58, 129, 168, 209, 212, 253

laissez faire   23, 27, 28, 34, 41, 44, 64, 169, 194, 195, 238

Latin America   52, 57, 63, 134

Lehman Brothers   11, 127, 151, 153, 163, 204

Leverage   11, 127, 151, 153, 163, 204

Liberal Democratic Party   95, 114

Liberalism   11, 12, 17, 115, 179, 196, 228, 254

Liberalization   67, 81, 82, 84, 111, 227–229

Liberals   31, 161, 196, 228, 255

Loans   54–58, 60, 62, 67,
    70, 71, 83, 88, 89, 100,
    109, 130, 131, 142, 145,
    146, 149, 150, 155, 157,
    159, 165, 166, 184, 205,
    249
Long Depression   248, 250,
    251, 254
Long Term Capital
    Management   155, 159,
    183
lost decade   8, 18, 29, 77, 78,
    81, 85, 86, 98, 112, 114

Madoff   11, 12, 35, 152,
    154, 182
Mahathir   63
Malaysia   53, 61, 63, 64,
    111, 130
market fundamentalism   3,
    10, 26, 27, 28, 44, 46,
    115, 255
Market society   10, 11, 40
Marshall Plan   128
Marshall, Alfred   12, 178,
    192, 194, 256
Marx, Karl   257
Merrill Lynch   11, 110, 145,
    150–153
Mexico   9, 42, 51, 52,
    56–60, 62, 64, 69, 134,
    220, 238

Mahbubani, Kishore   258
Mill, John   12, 178, 192,
    194, 195
Minsky, Hyman   167
Monetary policy   60, 81,
    82, 155, 156, 164, 211,
    249
moral hazards   206, 217
Moral values   45
Morgan Stanley   151, 185,
    204
Moscow   31, 250

naked CDS   203, 208
Napoleon   27
narrow banks   214
Nemesis   12
Neoliberal   11, 12, 17, 23,
    27, 30, 31, 34, 42, 161,
    179, 196–198, 227, 228,
    254
Neoliberalism   11, 12, 17,
    179, 196, 228, 254
New Economy   142, 252
New York   1, 27, 30, 167,
    177, 184, 188, 190,
    250
Nikon   102
Nokia   37, 105, 110
Nozick, Robert   197
NPL, non-performing loans,
    62, 88, 166

Obama   179, 204, 236, 237
OECD   9, 93, 126
one dimensional organization
   36
OPEC   80, 101, 126

Paris   55, 184, 186, 249,
   250
payment system   204, 213,
   215, 218
Pension funds   32, 145, 216
Peso crisis   17, 56, 66, 134
Peterson, Peter   131
Philippines   53, 61
Pigou, Arthur   12, 192, 195
Plato   12, 192
political legitimacy   189,
   190
Pope Benedict XVI   179
Production   4, 8, 83, 84, 99,
   101–104, 130, 142, 197,
   232, 245, 246, 253, 257
Productivity   5, 13, 14, 29,
   42, 79, 80, 90, 94, 97,
   99, 101–103, 105–107,
   109–111, 178, 184–186,
   188, 190, 250–253, 257

Reagan, Roland   23
Regulation   23, 24, 30, 43,
   45, 84, 86, 88, 94–97,
   139, 143, 144, 154–158,
   160–163, 167, 180–182,
   194, 198, 206, 213, 214,
   217, 218
Rich, John   177, 178
Rohatyn, Felix   190
Roubini, Nouriel   156
Royal Bank of Scotland   11,
   127, 141
Rubin, Robert   55, 64, 143
Russia   9, 30, 31, 42, 52

Sachs, Jeffery   196
Samsung   100, 105
Sandel, Michael   11, 39,
   180, 197
Savings and Loans   155
Schumpeter, Joseph   101,
   203, 257
Sen, Amartya   40, 193, 196
Shareholder   37, 100, 141,
   144, 146, 161, 162, 187,
   191, 198, 199, 204, 206,
   215, 218
Shimano   102
Singapore   23, 61, 77, 125,
   130, 181, 240
Smith, Adam   12, 41, 166,
   178, 180, 181, 192, 193,
   196, 257
social costs   24, 41
social legitimacy   178, 187,
   189, 190

Social values   11

societal resources   14, 259

Society-building   14

Solow, Robert   160, 164, 210

Soros, George   26, 33, 65, 67, 126, 157, 163

South Korea   4, 5, 8, 60, 61, 67, 100, 232

Soviet Union   24, 25, 27, 28, 41, 66, 140

Speculation   3, 6, 8, 16, 60, 103, 112, 143, 156, 158, 159, 167–169, 180, 181, 205, 210, 212, 249, 253

Stakeholder   37, 100, 187, 205, 238

Stanford   11

Stiglitz, Joseph   117, 188, 196

Subprime   10, 18, 109, 112, 129, 130, 141, 142, 160, 166, 180, 207, 249

Suharto   63

Summers, Lawrence   64, 220

Thailand   52, 53, 55, 60–62, 67, 69, 71, 89, 95

Thatcher, Margaret   23

Tobin, James   253

Tokyo   82, 91, 98, 104, 116

too big to fail   11, 207, 213

Toyota   102

Trade deficits   1, 3, 15, 60

Trade surplus   81, 82, 106, 235

UBS   145

Uncle Sam   19, 65, 66, 70, 108, 225, 239

USA, United States   1, 15, 23–25, 30, 31, 33, 40, 42, 44, 45, 51, 55, 59, 65, 66, 77, 78, 80, 82, 85, 99, 100, 107–110, 126, 127, 130, 131, 134, 141, 157, 178, 188, 190, 204, 208, 212, 226, 232–236, 238, 239, 244, 246, 248, 250, 253, 258, 259

value adding   79

Veblen, Thorstein   255

venture capital   217, 219, 239

Wall Street   9, 10, 30, 34, 35, 104, 115, 135, 140, 150–154, 160, 161, 168,

169, 177, 179, 181, 183,
184, 190, 198, 204, 208,
211, 221, 238, 251, 255,
259
Washington   26, 30, 58, 64,
65, 160, 220, 233, 237,
240
Washington Consensus   26,
30, 64

Waterloo   27
Wellington   27
World Bank   28, 55, 63,
184, 196
World War II   13, 23, 83,
103, 109, 112, 128,
225

ZTE   100